CHAUCER'S MAJOR TALES

Chaucer's Major Tales

MICHAEL HOY
AND
MICHAEL STEVENS

SCHOCKEN BOOKS · NEW YORK

First American edition published by Schocken Books 1983
10 9 8 7 6 5 4 3 2 1   83 84 85 86
© *Michael Hoy and Michael Stevens 1969*

Library of Congress Cataloging in Publication Data
Hoy, Michael
Chaucer's major tales.
Originally published: London: N. Bailey, 1969.
Bibliography: p.
Includes index.
1. Chaucer, Geoffrey, d. 1400. Canterbury tales.
I. Stevens, Michael. II. Title.
PR1874.H68   1983   821'.1   82-10419

Manufactured in the United States of America
ISBN 0-8052-3844-1 (hardcover)
0-8052-0734-1 (paperback)

FOR

OUR PARENTS AND MARY

Contents

Acknowledgements

IT IS readily apparent that in writing this book we owe a great debt to previous Chaucerian studies, not all of which will have received specific acknowledgement in the Notes or in the Bibliography. We would especially like to acknowledge the personal inspiration of two distinguished Chaucerian scholars, Mr A. C. Spearing and Professor J. J. Lawlor, who, as our respective tutors, fired our own enthusiasm for this period of English Literature. We gratefully acknowledge the encouragement and help we received from Mr Christopher Dixon, late Assistant Professor of English at Victoria College, University of Toronto, who suggested the lines the book should follow. We are indebted, too, to Mr Anthony Earl for his invaluable comment on problems of medieval philosophy, to Patrick and Marjorie Wilson for assistance with some historical material, and to Messrs. Faber and Faber for permission to reprint an extract from *The Waste Land*.

OAKHAM, Rutland.   M.J.H.
August 1969   M.S.

Preface

The criticism of medieval literature has undergone important changes in recent years. There is now an increased awareness of the complexity and sophistication of much medieval writing, and the modern critic no longer limits his reading to an appreciation of narrative and similar techniques. He has become more interested in the details of poetic texture and tonal variation, and in order to attempt an adequate assessment of these effects he has turned to the methods of close analysis which have characterized critical writing during the past thirty years. Criticism of Chaucer's poetry, in particular, has benefited greatly from this new confidence in modern critical methods which are, in essence, no less appropriate to fourteenth century literature than to that of the twentieth century. The advantages, together with some of the difficulties which face the critic who approaches medieval literature in this way are considered at length by A. C. Spearing in *Criticism and Medieval Poetry*.

The essays in this book try to provide this kind of close reading of selected parts of the *Canterbury Tales*. The ideas and facts which form the basis of each argument are presented in a form which attempts to provoke discussion and so extend the critical sensibility of the student both at 'A' Level and in the university. The essays do not offer a full picture of the historical and social background to Chaucer's art, but where an awareness of historical perspective is valuable then relevant information concerning contemporary life and customs is included in the critical argument. The importance of literary theory is also emphasized.

In order to provide this kind of information, we have drawn freely on medieval scholarship, selecting material which seems to us to be relevant to an understanding of the structure, meaning and poetic texture of the sections of the *Canterbury Tales* discussed.

The General Prologue

A faire felde ful of folke fonde I there bytwene,
Of alle maner of men þe mene and þe riche,
Worchyng and wandryng as þe worlde asketh
Some putten hem to þe plow pleyed ful selde,
In settyng and in sowyng swonken ful harde,
And wonnen that wastours with glotonye destruyeth.
    And some putten hem to pruyde apparailed hem þere-after,
In contenaunce of clothyng comen disgised.
    In prayers and in penance putten hem manye,
Al for loue of owre lorde lyueden ful streyte,
In hope forto haue heueneriche blisse . . .

(Langland: *Piers Plowman:* B Text,
Prologus, lines 17–27)

Pilgrims setting off in spring and summer to the shrine of Thomas à Becket at Canterbury would have been a familiar sight to Chaucer as he looked out across the South London countryside from the Aldgate house which he rented from 1374 to 1386. Pilgrimages were commonplace. Through them Englishmen were able to indulge their love of travel, fresh air and mixed good fellowship with its gossip, storytelling and music. A great deal of money was to be made out of these tourists of the Middle Ages, not only at the shrines themselves, but by the souvenir sellers and innkeepers along the routes; for the poorer pilgrims charitable guilds set up hostels. Manuals, which would vie with any of the modern travel brochures, gave practical advice on how one should conduct oneself on a pilgrimage, the kind of clothing to be worn, the foods to be avoided and helpful hints on money matters and rates of exchange. Some pilgrimages, particularly those to foreign shrines, were extremely hazardous, involving the penitent pilgrim in great hardships and discomfort, and it must not be forgotten that to go on a pilgrimage was one of the ways of earning a remission of the punishment in the life hereafter for sin committed on earth. The wealthy would sometimes bequeath money for pilgrimages to be carried out on their behalf after their death. It is not surprising that Chaucer somewhat ironically says of the Wife of Bath that :

> . . . thries hadde she been at Jerusalem;
> She hadde passed many a straunge strem;
> At Rome she hadde been, and at Boloigne,
> In Galice at Seint-Jame, and at Coloigne.
> (463–6)

And in this larger-than-life portrait one can detect the same kind of boastfulness that typifies the modern tourist who returns to brag about the number of countries visited. They had their serious aspects, to be sure, but certainly most of the domestic pilgrimages were joyous, carefree affairs with an air of carnival about them.

In his search for a means to provide a dramatic unifying

scheme for the publication of a collection of stories, of which it
has been conjectured he had already written those of the Knight,
the Second Nun and the Monk, nothing could suit Chaucer's
purpose more effectively than the setting of a pilgrimage with
all its opportunities for presenting such a wide cross-section of
contemporary life. To publish a collection of stories in this way
was no new idea; there had been already the *Thousand and One
Nights*, Boccaccio's *Filocolo*, *Decameron* and *Ameto*, and Gower's
Confessio Amantis. Chaucer would not necessarily have been
familiar with all these works, but the *Filocolo* may well have been
the source for 'The Franklin's Tale', and he would surely have
been in touch with Gower to whom he had dedicated his *Troilus
and Criseyde* and whose *Confessio* came out in 1390 when the
Canterbury Tales were well on the way. Chaucer had himself
experimented with the production of a set of tales within a
dramatic structure in *The Legend of Good Women*, but all these
examples look stereotyped and static when put alongside the
Canterbury Tales in which Chaucer's originality and imagination
brought to life such a diverse range of characters.

Nevertheless, with all this emphasis on his popular appeal
and 'modernity', it would be quite wrong to think of Chaucer
as a twentieth-century writer who found himself in the Middle
Ages by mistake. All his work is assuredly set within the framework of the intellectual and philosophical thought of his day,
and one significant aspect of that thought, emphasized by St
Thomas Aquinas, was a concern for unity. The background to
the first half of the thirteenth century is a story of student revolt.
Dissatisfied with their impoverished conditions in one of Europe's
wealthiest capitals, in which the higher clergy formed an intellectual aristocracy, the Parisian scholars eagerly turned to the
secular and free-thinking philosophy of Averroës; and it was this
permissive society which the cynical Jean de Meung portrayed
in his continuation of the *Roman de la Rose*. Chastity was out-
moded, theology was a myth, and the cry of, 'Thou, Nature,
art my goddess' was as much on the lips of this avant garde
community of the Middle Ages as in Jacobean or more recent
times. Into this intellectual ferment was injected the more
rationalistic theology of St Thomas Aquinas. Although St
Thomas leaves much to *mysterium* and the belief that ultimate
truth is revealed only by Revelation, he acknowledges that human

reason helps to clarify the articles of faith, even if it does not provide direct proof of them. He was at home

> . . . in a social order dependent upon the aristocracy and the urban citizenry. . . . Thomas's cosmos had been built as a city-state by a noble God who was its *rector civitatis*, monarch and law-giver. The Universe, like the Kingdom of God (represented on earth by the Church) was therefore an ordered society, *ordinata civitas*.[1]

This medieval philosophy reflects the changing of the social system to what E. Panofsky describes as an 'urban professionalism' in which 'the priest and the layman, the poet and the lawyer, the scholar and the artisan could get together on terms of near equality',[2] and this can be detected in the *Canterbury Tales* in several ways, not only through the unified dramatic structure of the tales themselves, but also in the concern taken by the poet to suit each tale to its teller. Although the connection between some of the tales and their tellers as described in 'The General Prologue' is somewhat tenuous, most of the tales which are discussed in the following chapters, with the exception of that of the Clerk, are ideally suited to the character who tells them. The Knight who was 'ever honoured for his worthiness' appropriately tells the first Tale and it is right it should be one of chivalry and romance. The Franklin who:

> At sessiouns ther was he lord and sire;
> Ful ofte tyme he was knyght of the shire.
> (355-6)

was ideally suited to act as a mediator between the fractious pilgrims and, although not of the Knight's noble blood, was a member of the gentry, so that his similarly chivalric romance is appropriately pitched at a lower level than 'The Knight's Tale', but in the same Courtly Love setting. The sentimental but wholly Christian story which the Prioress tells of the little child is quite in accord with the modest, demure creature, sincere in her religion, who

> . . . wolde wepe, if that she saugh a mous
> Kaught in a trappe, if it were deed or bledde.
> (144-5)

The cupidity and violence in 'The Pardoner's Tale' of the three rioters and their quest for Death is suited to such an obsequious

character who 'with feyned flaterye and japes . . . made the person and the peple his apes'. For some reason the character of the Nun's Priest is not described at all in 'The General Prologue' but the tone of his Tale with its digressions on pre-destination and free will is quite in harmony with what we should expect from one of the lesser clergy travelling with the Prioress, and who admits in the Tale he tells:

> But I ne kan nat bulte it to the bren
> As kan the hooly doctour Augustyn,
> Or Boece, or the Bisshop Bradwardyn . . .
> *(NPT* 3240–2)

Aquinas was an Aristotelian to whom 'unity' and 'goodness' were the same. As Professor Heer says:

> God, Architect, Artist, and Monarch, himself guarantees the goodness, truth and beauty of the being and order of the world. Being is good, ordo bonitatis; all things imitate the Divine Goodness which exists in simple wholeness, and strive, according to their ability, to be like him.[3]

In an interesting essay[4] P. Mroczkowski shows how this idea of goodness and beauty is also the same as conformity to an ideal, and that the description of beauty in portraits of human characters was generally aimed to satisfy a reader's own particular set of stock responses as to how a particular character or type should be presented. This aesthetic theory is also linked with the rules of rhetoric as laid down by Geoffroi de Vinsauf, and certainly the rhetorical figure of *descriptio* arose naturally out of the device known as *amplificatio* which largely accounted for the lengthy digressions and prolixity of style in medieval literature. It was expected that there should be unity in these descriptions and certain requirements had to be fulfilled in order to make a portrait complete. Chaucer, of course, does not follow the rules as slavishly as do other medieval writers. In 'The Nun's Priest's Tale', for instance, he dealt with the laws of the *Nova Poetria* of Vinsauf in a very casual manner, and it is the same with the aesthetic unity of his portraits. Even when he is talking about a character such as the Prioress, and appears to accept many of the required conventional features so characteristic of the French Romances, he describes

> Hir nose tretys, hir eyen greye as glas,
> Hir mouth ful smal, and therto softe and reed;
> But sikerly she hadde a fair forheed;
> It was almoost a spanne brood, I trowe . . .
>
> (152–5)

But here in the final line he introduces the touch of irony which does not accord with a reader's stock response to such a 'good' character: a broad forehead was a sign of physical beauty, which therefore implied a degree of worldliness not entirely appropriate to such a religious character whose forehead should have been completely covered by her wimple.

As Northrop Frye[5] suggests, it is interesting to notice that after the *Canterbury Tales* no such varied survey of human nature in a single unified literary work is to be found again until Burton's *Anatomy of Melancholy* of 1621, in another age of rational belief. This comparison between the fourteenth century and the seventeenth and early eighteenth centuries in this respect can be brought into even clearer focus when one considers the relationship between the various art forms of the two periods. Henry Adams points out how the method used by St Thomas Aquinas in formulating the structure of his theology was the same as that of the architects of Amiens cathedral,

> and the result was an art marked by the singular unity, which endured and served its purpose until man changed his attitude towards the universe. . . . Granted a Church, Saint Thomas's Church was the most expressive that man has made, and the great Gothic cathedrals were its most complete expression.[6]

James Sutherland[7] draws a similar comparison between the literature and art of the eighteenth century when he compares Pope's unrealistic treatment of nature in 'Windsor Forest' to a woodcarving by Grinling Gibbons. Sutherland also says that 'the poet aims at achieving the sort of unified impression that he was himself accustomed to receiving from contemporary architecture',[8] and he quotes Pope's

> Thus when we view some well-proportion'd dome,
> (The world's just wonder, and ev'n thine, O Rome!)
> No single parts unequally surprize;
> All comes united to th'admiring eyes;
> No monstrous height, or breadth, or length appear;
> The whole at once is bold, and regular.

In each case the exceptions can also be paralleled: the Gothic cathedrals had their gargoyles, and Chaucer's Cook his mormal on his shin, and the Summoner 'the knobbes sittynge on his chekes'.

The decorative eighteenth century produced the Yahoos and the harsh satirical works of Hogarth. Hugh of St Victor, the most liberal of the Victorite humanists, emphasized the necessity for richness and variety in beauty which, of course, is exactly what Chaucer provides in presenting so many diversified aspects of the world scene.

> Whan that Aprill with his shoures soote
> The droghte of March hath perced to the roote,
> And bathed every veyne in swich licour
> Of which vertu engendred is the flour;
> Whan Zephirus eek with his sweete breeth
> Inspired hath in every holt and heeth
> The tendre croppes, and the yonge sonne
> Hath in the Ram his halve cours yronne,
> And smale foweles maken melodye,
> That slepen al the nyght with open ye
> (So priketh hem nature in hir corages);
> Thanne longen folk to goon on pilgrimages,
> And palmeres for to seken straunge strondes,
> To ferne halwes, kowthe in sondry londes;
> And specially from every shires ende
> Of Engelond to Caunterbury they wende,
> The hooly blisful martir for to seke,
> That hem hath holpen whan that they were seeke.
>   (1–18)

This conventional opening, in the *Roman de la Rose* tradition, appears to have little connection with the portraits that follow, none of which, except for the passing reference to the Reeve who lived 'ful faire upon an heeth' among green trees, is directly related to a natural environment, and we are given surprisingly few geographical details of the journey to Canterbury. However, it has been pointed out by Arthur W. Hoffman that in these opening lines 'springtime is characterized in terms of procreation'[9] and there is a strongly suggestive physical tone in the description of the masculine April, whose 'shoures soote' have 'perced' the feminine March; it is Nature that 'priketh' the

hearts of the birds 'that slepen al the nyght with open ye'. There is generated—Chaucer himself uses the word 'engendred'—in these opening lines a great physical vitality which prevails throughout the whole of 'The General Prologue' in the descriptions of the characters. It is interesting to compare as John Speirs has suggested[10] the liveliness of the opening lines of the *Canterbury Tales* with the aimlessness and frustration of the opening of 'The Waste Land':

> April is the cruellest month, breeding
> Lilacs out of the dead land, mixing
> Memory and desire, stirring
> Dull roots with spring rain.
> Winter kept us warm, covering
> Earth in forgetful snow, feeding
> A little life with dried tubers.
> Summer surprised us, coming over the Starnbergersee
> With a shower of rain; we stopped in the colonnade,
> And went on in sunlight, into the Hofgarten,
> And drank coffee, and talked for an hour.

This is passive and sterile ('And drank coffee, and talked for an hour'); there is none of the association between man and nature which is such a characteristic unity to be found in the active and creative lines of the opening to 'The General Prologue' ('Thanne longen folk to goon on pilgrimages'). Chaucer emphasizes this association by his repetitive use of the word 'corage' in lines 11 and 22. In the first instance with reference to the natural world of the birds 'that slepen al the nyght with open ye' and in the second with reference to the pilgrims themselves who are described as being 'with ful devout corage'. There is also some religious significance in that this is the season of the year associated by Christian tradition with Eastertide and the time of man's Redemption, which closely links this apparently conventional opening with the idea of pilgrimage for, as Professor Donaldson says, 'Chaucer uses the spiritual act of pilgrimage to reveal the whole Christian principle of regeneration.' The possibility revealed in the opening of 'The General Prologue' is 'that the Divine love that revives the dead world annually is large enough to countenance the whole paradox of man's nature.'[11] These are the two voices of the Prologue in which, as Charles Muscatine says: 'April, sweet rains, and song birds, set beside pilgrimage

and the holy blissful martyr, establish that double theme of nature and supernature, natural value and spiritual, which is at the heart of the whole work.'[12] The world of Nature and that of Grace ultimately unite in Chaucer's vision.

'Wel nyne and twenty in a compaignye, of sondry folk' gathered at the Tabard Inn on the night before the pilgrimage. Chaucer does, in fact, refer to thirty pilgrims and, with a characteristic touch of humour, also includes himself along with such rogues as the Reeve, the Miller, the Summoner and the Pardoner. Neither the Canon nor his Yeoman is mentioned in 'The General Prologue' for they join the party in rather suspicious circumstances later on at Boughton under Blee. The Canon disappears but his Yeoman remains so that, together with the Host, thirty-three pilgrims actually complete the journey to Canterbury.

When one starts to consider the comprehensive survey of human nature spread out in 'The General Prologue' one cannot but agree with Dryden, who remarks in his *Preface* to the *Fables*, which include verse paraphrases of several of the *Canterbury Tales*, that 'there is such a variety of game springing up before me that I am distracted in my choice, and know not which to follow. 'Tis sufficient to say, according to the proverb, that here is God's plenty.'[13] Plenty, indeed. It would, of course, have been inappropriate to include the two extremes of the social classes amongst the pilgrims, and Chaucer would not have been so unmindful of decorum as to include either royalty and aristocracy or the very humble rustics among his party. Nevertheless, it is difficult to think of many other omissions and, whereas his characters can be grouped into fairly well-defined social categories,[14] there is a complete individuality, both in the physical descriptions and in the descriptions of the various personalities and temperaments of the pilgrims.

Appropriately enough the first to be described is the Knight. Chaucer here gives us an idealized, conventional picture of a crusader with all the much-admired qualities of chivalry and romance so strongly emphasized by his valorous exploits overseas and by his Christianity; so eager was he to join the pilgrimage in order to fulfil a vow, that his tunic was still 'al

bismotered with his habergeon'. The Knight's son, the Squire, shows the same devotion to military exploits expected from someone of his class, but that is as far as the similarity goes, for he is very much a gay Lothario.

The professional class is represented by the Sergeant at Law, a high-ranking barrister in line to be appointed a judge, extremely well-versed in the law of the land, but who is not above twisting that law to suit his own purposes. Another member of a learned profession is the Doctor of Physik, who was much-respected for his knowledge of astronomy and his awareness of the vital influence of the planets on the well-being of his patients. Travelling with the Sergeant is one of the world's social climbers in the person of the Franklin, who is out to impress as much as he is easily impressed himself.

Not only are the different social groups so plainly defined but the various levels within each of these groups are also clearly distinguished, and this is particularly noticeable with all the characters representing the commercial classes. At the top must come the Merchant himself, expensively dressed in his 'Flaundryssh bever hat', one of the flourishing wholesale wool exporters who, in addition to the profit made from selling his goods on the European market, had a lucrative sideline in currency exchanges. The Haberdasher, Carpenter, Weaver, Dyer and Tapestry Maker were all members of the same social or religious gild, and represented the lower reaches of city commercial life, but they did employ their own cook and

> Wel semed ech of hem a fair burgeys
> To sitten in a yeldehalle on a deys.
> (369–70)

Between these two extremes of London traders must come the Wife of Bath, a middle-class provincial representing the manufacturers of the famous West of England cloth. She was obviously a person of some standing in the parish ('wif ne was ther noon / That to the offrynge bifore hire sholde goon') and she was so skilful in her cloth-making that 'She passed hem of Ypres and of Gaunt'. Within this class we can place another West Countryman, the Shipman, who owned his own boat and whose seamanship and navigational skill matched his swashbuckling exploits ashore and afloat.

Coming down the social scale we reach the coarse, swaggering Miller, who probably owned his own mill but who is one of the most disreputable members of the whole company, and with his sparring partner, the Reeve, we have representatives from the administrative side of the feudal manor. The Manciple as an under steward in one of the legal colleges would have been on much the same social level, but a good deal higher than that of the hard-working Cook with his cancerous sores. The lowest of all must have been the Plowman, a villein, renting his strips of land from the feudal manor in return for which he would have had to labour on the domain. But it is significant to notice that whereas Chaucer gives us the idealized portrait of the Knight at the top of the social ladder, so also at the lowest level he provides another idealized portrait:

> A trewe swynkere and a good was he,
> Lyvynge in pees and parfit charitee.
> God loved he best . . .
>
> (531–3)

which befits the brother of the Parson.

And so to the religious characters. Here again one can appreciate Chaucer's skill not only in delineating particular individual characters but also his ability in distinguishing between the various categories within each group, and this is, perhaps, more difficult with the characters of religion where rank is relatively unimportant. The idealized portrait of the Parson is presented in a rather different way from the other idealized portraits in 'The General Prologue'. As well as being told what the Parson did, we are also told what the Parson did not do, and in this way Chaucer is enabled to show by implication the way in which many of the less worthy clerics of his day actually behaved. In spite of his poverty, the Parson did not neglect his parochial duties and supplement his stipend by obtaining office in a Chantry where his only task would be the saying of a certain number of Masses. Chaucer's Parson practises what he preaches: 'He taughte, but first he folwed it hymselve.' Another difference with this portrait is that it is the only one in which a sustained metaphor is used to describe the character, and it is, of course, effective that the conventional pastoral metaphor of the priest as shepherd should be used for the brother of the Plowman.

The lowly origins of the Parson are offset by the coquetry of the Prioress who 'peyned hire to countrefete cheere of court', but we need not lay too much emphasis on Chaucer's ironical hints at excessive worldliness in the character of the Prioress. She was not a member of a strictly contemplative order, but would have been called upon to fulfil the role of a hostess and a schoolmistress, so that the reference to her attention to matters of etiquette and her table manners are quite appropriate, and with her musical ability and academic French she is shown to possess those qualities to be desired in a teacher of young ladies.

The Monk was a member of a contemplative religious order and bound by vows of poverty and chastity; so in portraying this bloated prelate with his stable full of expensively caparisoned horses, his disregard for the conclusions of theology and learning, his lavish dress and predilection for fat roast swan, Chaucer is radical in his criticism of medieval religious practices. The true monks of the thirteenth century were expected to be removed from worldly vanities, but in spite of their vows of poverty some monasteries were extremely wealthy establishments tending to foster a religious aristocracy with no contact with the people. To overcome this remoteness the orders of mendicant friars were founded, but many of their members quickly succumbed to the temptations of the flesh, and Chaucer's portrait describes one such who 'knew the tavernes wel in every toun' and whose absolutions could be a profitable business because 'Men moote yeve silver to the povre freres'. Although like the Monk, but unlike the Parson or the Clerk, he is well-dressed 'lyk a maister or a pope', nevertheless Chaucer does not adopt such a strong tone of censure with the Friar. He is more on a par with the Prioress, for he too could 'synge and pleyen on a rote', was physically attractive and inclined to be a little affected: 'Somwhat he lipsed, for his wantownesse'.

Chaucer's severest strictures are kept for his portraits of the lay associates of the Church, namely the Summoner and his companion the Pardoner. After referring with some irony to his 'fyr-reed cherubynnes face', Chaucer's description of the Summoner's physical appearance is of a unity with the description of his character, and it is for him that Chaucer reserves his most repugnant details:

As hoot he was and lecherous as a sparwe,
With scalled browes blake and piled berd.
Of his visage children were aferd.
Ther nas quyk-silver, lytarge, ne brymstoon,
Boras, ceruce, ne oille of tartre noon;
Ne oynement that wolde clense and byte,
That hym myghte helpen of his whelkes white,
Nor of the knobbes sittynge on his chekes.
Wel loved he garleek, oynons, and eek lekes,
And for to drynken strong wyn, reed as blood;
Thanne wolde he speke and crie as he were wood.
And whan that he wel dronken hadde the wyn,
Thanne wolde he speke no word but Latyn.

(626–38)

The long, leering vowel sounds of the opening lead into the
clipped alliterative snarl of 'browes blake and piled berd', to be
followed by the emotive appeal: 'Of his visage children were
aferd.' This is the only reference to children in 'The General
Prologue' and is doubly effective when one considers the sentimental attitude towards them in the literature of the Middle
Ages. The rhetorical device of *amplificatio*, giving the encyclo-
paedic list of unavailing remedies, and the details of the Summoner's unsophisticated diet and intemperance, convey
Chaucer's feeling of revulsion, which he continues for another
thirty lines. He does, perhaps, soften the blow a little at the very
end by showing up the Summoner as a complete buffoon with
his garland on his head, and his buckler made of cake. The same
forceful language is not used to describe the Pardoner, but the
implications in the contrast between his effeminacy and the
Summoner's overt masculinity are no less pointed, and in his
description of the Pardoner's unscrupulous methods Chaucer
makes his own views quite plain.

Inevitably one wonders what Chaucer's personal attitude was
to the Church in the England of his day.[15] From his balanced
descriptions in 'The General Prologue' it seems that he tolerantly
accepted the position as he found it. Over one third of 'The
General Prologue' is devoted to matters of religion; but of the
thirty characters that are described on this pilgrimage to a Saint's
shrine in Canterbury Cathedral, all of whom presumably professed and called themselves Christians, only three were pre-

sented as true upholders of the faith—and two of these were laymen.

One cannot deny that standards of clerical behaviour were low; but at a time when all church services were conducted in Latin, and when the general level of literacy was poor, the Parish Priest was almost entirely responsible for the guidance and instruction of his flock. He had to set an example; hence the force of Chaucer's remark:

> That if gold ruste, what shal iren do?
> For if a preest be foul, on whom we truste,
> No wonder is a lewed man to ruste.
>
> (500–2)

Chaucer is not alone in drawing attention to the clerical backsliders of his time, and the picture painted by his contemporary Langland in *Piers Plowman* similarly describes a priest who knows his rhymes of Robin Hood better than his Paternoster and who is

> . . . occupied eche day haliday and other,
> With ydel tales atte ale and otherwhile in cherches. . .[16]

The influence of the Black Death which ravaged the country from 1348 onwards, wiping out whole communities and disrupting the economic and social life of England, is referred to in detail in the chapter on 'The Pardoner's Tale'. Its implications are no less apparent in 'The General Prologue' where we have such a comprehensive survey of the people who lived in those violent and turbulent times in the midst of so much death. It was an age of extremes: the gaudy, colourful spectacle of heraldic pageantry on the one hand, encouraging a philosophy which gave undue prominence to the here and now, and on the other, the gloomy preoccupation with death and the fear of eternal damnation in the life hereafter, tormented by foul fiends and devils. The threat of excommunication was a very real one, for to die unshriven and deprived of the rites of Holy Church was to die condemned to the fire and brimstone of purgatory. With the power to administer this threat, the Church, for some, had a great influence; and if the alternative salvation could be bought, many people were prepared to pay the price. There is abundant evidence of this in 'The General Prologue': the very

pilgrimage itself was a means of atonement, 'Men moote yeve silver to the povre freres', and money poured into the pockets of the Summoner and the Pardoner who:

> Upon a day he gat hym moore moneye
> Than that the person gat in monthes tweye.
> (703-4)

We are told that

> Of cursyng oghte ech gilty man him drede,
> For curs wol slee right as assoillyng savith . . .
> (660-1)

A strong sense of judgement pervades the whole of 'The General Prologue' and with it there is implied the acceptance of authority whether it be Divinely imposed through the ministers of the Church or through the officers of the State. In a feudal society this was, of course, more readily accepted than it would have been at other times. Even the pilgrims themselves, from the highest to the low, accept the authority of the Host acknowledging him as 'governour' and they are told by him that,

> . . . whoso wole my juggement withseye
> Shal paye al that we spenden by the weye.
> (805-6)

And so,

> . . . by oon assent
> We been acorded to his juggement.
> (817-18)

But only fifteen lines later the Host sees fit to repeat his earlier comment almost word for word:

> Whoso be rebel to my juggement
> Shal paye for al that by the wey is spent.
> (833-4)

By contrast the Monk flouts the authority of the Founder of his Order, but the Sergeant administers the laws of the kingdom, and the Summoner frightens everyone with his 'questio quid juris' and his 'Significavit'.

In comparison with this tone of judgement there is also a unifying theme of love expressed in all its different connotations:

the love of 'chivalrie, trouthe and honour' of the Knight, the sexual love of the Squire, the altruistic love of the Parson and his brother the Plowman, and the Prioress with her 'Amor Vincit Omnia'. Paradoxically there are also the opposite forms revealed by the Monk's self-indulgent love of 'venerie' and fat swan and the Franklin's similar love of Epicurean delights.[17]

All these contrasts reflect the extremes of the times in which Chaucer lived. Life in the Middle Ages was much more clear-cut than it is today, so that we are constantly aware of these opposites: not only of life and death, salvation and damnation, but also of day and night, brightness and darkness, warmth and cold, health and sickness and spring and winter. It is with this seasonal contrast that 'The General Prologue' opens, and at the very end of the introductory lines of the opening eulogy to spring with all its *joie de vivre* and bursting good health, we are reminded that it was the 'hooly blisful martir' who cured the pilgrims 'whan that they were seeke'.

The contrast in appearance and character of the Knight and his son, the Squire, has already been referred to, but the Squire's vitality is certainly the nearest to the Nature of the opening lines of 'The General Prologue':

> Embrouded was he, as it were a meede
> Al ful of fresshe floures, whyte and reede,
> Syngynge he was, or floytynge, al the day;
> He was as fressh as is the month of May.
>
> (89–92)

J. Huizinga writes:

> The lasting vogue of the pastoral genre towards the end of the Middle Ages implies a reaction against the ideal of courtesy. Weary of the complicated formalism of chivalrous love, the aristocratic soul re-nounces the overstrung pretension of heroism in love, and praises rural life as the escape from it. The new, or rather revived, bucolic ideal remains essentially an erotic one.[18]

No better example of this can be found than in the reactionary pastorality of the Squire, so reminiscent of the 'flower people' of more recent times, contrasted as it is with the chivalric ideals of the Knight.

The hyperbolic descriptions of the physical attributes of so many of the characters emphasize the unifying theme of vitality,

the tone of which is set by the opening lines: the Monk with his eyes 'that stemed as a forneys of a leed', even the Friar was as strong as a champion, but the ascetic Clerk, to point the contrast, 'looked holwe'. The Shipman was 'a good felawe' when it came to drinking (stealing the wine into the bargain) and one who threw his adversaries overboard. The Wife of Bath, five times married, with an impressive record of foreign travel, is one of Chaucer's most vital characters:

> In felaweshipe wel koude she laughe and carpe.
> Of remedies of love she knew per chaunce,
> For she koude of that art the olde daunce.
>
> (474–6)

The Miller was a prize fighter able to lift any door off its hinges, but by contrast, his antagonist, the Reeve, was 'a sclendre colerik man'; and finally the lecherous Summoner with his droning bass voice is contrasted with the effeminate Pardoner whose voice was 'as smal as hath a goot' and 'No berd hadde he, ne nevere sholde have'. It is through these two closing portraits that the double definition of the pilgrimage is highlighted by revealing the obvious lack of love in the lives of the lustful Summoner and the impotent Pardoner as they ironically sing 'Com hider, love, to me!'

One cannot refer to Chaucer's two-fold interpretation of the whole structure of the pilgrimage without also considering the double persona adopted by the poet himself. I have mentioned this in greater detail in the chapter on 'The Franklin's Tale', but it is no less apparent in 'The General Prologue', although here there is no narrator behind whom Chaucer can hide when he wishes to make some provocative comment. There is, of course, the Host, one character not yet referred to, who is an essential agent in providing the dramatic unity of the whole work. However, apart from contriving the choice of the Knight as the first story-teller, and asserting his authority over the pilgrims, which they are all prepared to acknowledge, Harry Bailly makes no significant comment in 'The General Prologue'. One is, nevertheless, conscious of a powerful masculine personality well able to direct and manage the social side of the pilgrimage. The Host's character emerges in a subtly different way from those of the other pilgrims; and, of course, he did not join the com-

pany as one of those who 'longen to goon on pilgrimages' but as a
professional hotelier anxious to have the opportunity of providing
accommodation for the party on their return from Canterbury.
In engineering the return to Southwark he, therefore, provides a
further degree of unity by bringing the story full circle.[19] Here,
then, Chaucer is on his own, but he makes it quite clear before
the end of 'The General Prologue' that Chaucer the narrator
reading aloud to his courtly and sophisticated audience is not the
same creature as Chaucer the pilgrim. As narrator he is prepared
to recount the circumstances of the pilgrimage and to give details of the dress and appearance of the pilgrims, but lest any of
his listeners should take offence at anything he says or implies,
he reminds them that

> Whoso shal telle a tale after a man,
> He moot reherce as ny as evere he kan
> Everich a word, if it be in his charge,
> Al speke he never so rudeliche and large,
> Or ellis he moot telle his tale untrewe,
> Or feyne thyng, or fynde wordes newe
> (731–6)

and he goes on to quote classical and Biblical authority for his
excuse. In addition to shielding Chaucer from any obloquy, this
insistence upon fact enables him to bring his portraits to life
and to prevent them from being the stereotyped and static
figures of convention. There were surely no stifled yawns among
the courtly listeners of his own day, and the popularity of his
portraits has scarcely diminished over the 600 years to our own
time when they have been presented on radio and television and
in a stage musical production.

'The General Prologue' is a social and historical record of the
Middle Ages and we can learn much of the way of life in those
days from the habits and customs of the pilgrims as Chaucer
describes them to us: the chivalric virtues of the Knight and his
son the Squire who 'carf biforn his fader at the table'; the Merchant who 'wolde the see were kept for any thyng Bitwixe
Middelburgh and Orewelle'; the Sergeant at Law whose con-
veyancing of property was so skilful that 'Al was fee symple to
hym in effect'; the Doctor of Physik who 'Wel koude he fortunen
the ascendent—Of his ymages for his pacient'; the Wife of Bath

who 'Housbondes at chirche dore she hadde fyve'; the Miller who
had 'a thombe of gold, pardee'; the Manciple with his reference to
buying on credit 'wheither that he payde or took by taille'. All
these and many other examples provide a fascinating insight
into the medieval world picture, but it is not solely on account
of its historical interest that 'The General Prologue' commands
our attention. Chaucer's determination not 'to telle his tale
untrewe' provides us with a gallery of universally recognizable
characters: the flowery youthful Squire, the coquettish and
affected Prioress, the social-climbing Franklin, the much too
worldly Monk, the swaggering Shipman and many others. Of
course there is a great deal of exaggeration so that some of the
portraits appear as caricatures, but this is used for emphasis and
does not detract from the reality of the characters described.
Poetically this is extremely effective, especially when Chaucer
is making his many comparisons through the use of simile and
metaphor: the Monk's bridle 'gynglen . . . as dooth the chapel
belle' or 'His eyen stepe, and rollynge in his heed, / That stemed
as a forneys of a leed': the Friar whose 'nekke whit was as the
flour-de-lys'; the Franklin in whose house it 'snewed . . . of mete
and drynke'. Such hyperbole also enlivens the verse with delightful touches of humour as when he says of the coverchiefs of
the Wife of Bath's headdress that 'I dorste swere they weyeden
ten pound.'

   I have tried to show how both comparisons and contrasts
have paradoxically contributed to the unified structure of 'The
General Prologue', and it is also in the adroit juxtaposing of the
characters themselves that we may observe another of the ways
in which Chaucer prevents his survey from becoming a mere
static catalogue. He does not group the portraits together according to any defined classification; ecclesiastic, lay, commercial,
high-ranking and humble characters jostle each other with easy
familiarity, but this is not to say that the arrangement is hap-
hazard: the significance of the juxtaposition of the Knight and
the Squire, the Parson and the Plowman and several others has
already been commented upon. Some of the descriptions are of
considerable length, others of only a line or two; some characters
have their physical features described in detail, others their dress,
while others still, such as the Parson, are not physically described
at all, but some fifty lines devoted entirely to a character study.

There is variety, too, in the language; for the most part it is informal and colloquial as befits the rather naïve simplicity of Chaucer the narrator, but the verse can be lyrical as in the lilting opening lines, or it can convey the necessary scornful tone when used to describe a character such as the Summoner.

In the midst of all the contrasts and comparisons, the variety and the plenty, there is a unity in 'The General Prologue' which provides the appropriate introduction for the whole dramatic unifying framework of the *Canterbury Tales*.

The Knight's Tale

The firste stok, fader of gentilesse—
What man that claymeth gentil for to be
Must folowe his trace, and alle his wittes dresse
Vertu to sewe, and vyces for to flee.
                    (Chaucer: 'Gentilesse': lines 1–4)

At the Host's request the pilgrims draw lots to decide who should tell the first tale, and it is no great coincidence that 'the cut fil to the Knyght' whom Chaucer portrays as representing the highest ideals of medieval Christian chivalry. He combines in his person and his office all the virtue of a devout Christian, of a respected member of the nobility and of a military commander skilled in the use of arms and experienced in foreign travel. As one would expect in the Age of Chivalry there is great emphasis laid upon the glory of war, but it must be remembered that the wars he fought in were the Holy Crusades. The Knight, we are told, 'loved chivalrie, Trouthe and honour, fredom and curteisie' (*Gen Prol* 45–6). He is, therefore, a particularly appropriate character to start the series off and to set a pattern for all the stories that follow.

The elevated rhetorical style so appropriate to this 'noble storie' and to its dignified narrator is adopted at the outset and maintained throughout, and is a great contrast to the colloquial informality of 'The General Prologue' and many of the other tales. This Tale opens with the conventional rhetorical reference to authority ('as olde stories tellen us') and we are straightaway introduced to the epic character of Duke Theseus who, like the Knight himself, is returning victorious from the wars when he is waylaid by the Theban wives. But even in the compassion shown by Theseus for their predicament, very little warmth of character is displayed. It is all very formal, with the introduction of a Senecan revenge theme and with the wailing women themselves behaving more like the Chorus in a classical drama than as fellow human beings who engage our sympathy. After addressing Theseus as

> . . . 'Lord, to whom Fortune hath yiven
> Victorie, and as a conqueror to lyven . . .'
> (915–16)

'the eldeste lady' goes on to say of their own plight:

> 'For, certes, lord, ther is noon of us alle,
> That she ne hath been a duchesse or a queene.

> Now be we caytyves, as it is wel seene,
> Thanked be Fortune and hire false wheel,
> That noon estaat assureth to be weel.'
>
> (922–6)

The wives in their appeal to Theseus first mention their loss of social status, not their grief at the death of their husbands whose corpses have been desecrated. This degradation is at the heart of medieval tragedy and is

> The harm of hem that stoode in heigh degree,
> And fillen so that ther nas no remedie
> To brynge hem out of hir adversitee.
> For certein, whan that Fortune list to flee,
> Ther may no man the cours of hire withholde.
>
> (*Mk T* 1992–6)

With all the formality and ritual of tragic drama we are introduced right at the beginning to the central theme of 'The Knight's Tale' with the noble duke 'In al his wele and in his mooste pride' suddenly being made aware of the sufferings of others.

The turbulence of life in the Middle Ages with its emphasis both on the joys of living and the dread of death is reflected time and again in the writings of Chaucer. Pessimism alternates with optimism in an age when people were 'Now up, now doun, as boket in a welle' (1533) and when the glitter of chivalric pomp vied with the gloom of premature death and eternal damnation. It is the difference between the colourful description of Theseus's equipment:

> The rede statue of Mars, with spere and targe,
> So shyneth in his white baner large,
> That alle the feeldes glyteren up and doun . . .
>
> (975–7)

and the dismal forebodings in the description of the temple of the same 'myghty Mars the rede' with

> The pykepurs, and eek the pale Drede;
> The smylere with the knyf under the cloke . . .
>
> (1998–9)

This immediately follows the account of the statue of Venus with her

... rose gerland, fressh and wel smellynge;
Above hir heed hir dowves flikerynge.
(1961-2)

'The Knight's Tale' was almost certainly written before
Chaucer had conceived the idea of the whole scheme of the
Canterbury Tales. In the Prologue to *The Legend of Good Women*,
where he lists some of his completed works, Chaucer mentions
one about 'al the love of Palamon and Arcite of Thebes'. The Tale
would probably have been written about the same time as *Troilus
and Criseyde* and also his prose version of the *Consolatione Philosophiae* of Boethius, each of which is of some significance in considering 'The Knight's Tale'. The story of Palamon and Arcite is
derived from a long romantic epic poem *Il Teseide* by Giovanni
Boccaccio whose *Il Filostrato* had also provided the material for
Troilus and Criseyde, and as with his treatment of the 'Teseide'
for the earlier poem, so Chaucer's treatment of the source of
'The Knight's Tale' is principally to medievalize Boccaccio's
work. One of the means of achieving this medievalization was to
infuse his version with the Boethian philosophy that had such
an appeal in the Middle Ages with its pessimistic concern for
'the Wreched Engendrynge of Mankynde' (*LGW*, G Text, 414).

Inevitably the uncomplicated plot of 'The Knight's Tale'
prompts the philosophical question of why Providence, who is
all good, should allow one of two cousins of identical circumstances of birth and fortune to die, while the other is allowed to
remain 'Lyvynge in blisse, in richesse, and in heele' (3102). It is
the same question which the sixth-century Roman thinker Anicius
Manlius Boethius had considered in his *De Consolatione Philosophiae*, which takes the form of a dialogue between Boethius and
his 'nurse' Philosophy. After proving to him that both blessed-
ness and God are the chiefest good, Philosophy goes on to say:

> Providence is the very Divine reason itself, seated in the highest
> Prince, which disposeth of all things. But Fate is a disposition in-
> herent in changeable things, by which Providence connecteth all
> things in their due order. Perceivest thou now what followeth?' [she
> asked]. 'What?' [said I]. 'That' [quoth she], 'all manner of fortune is
> good.'

And after proving that nothing happens by chance, Philosophy
goes on:

'Ought, then, by parity of reason, all things to be just because He is just who willed them to be? That is not so either. For to be good involves Being, to be just involves an act. For him being and action are identical; to be good and to be just are one and the same for Him. But being and action are not identical for us, for we are not simple. For us, then, goodness is not the same thing as justice, but we all have the same sort of Being in virtue of our existence. Therefore all things are good, but all things are not just. Finally, good is general, but just is a species, and this species does not apply to all. Wherefore some things are just, others are something else, but all things are good.'[1]

These stoical views influenced Chaucer considerably and he incorporates them in several of his works, but none with more irony than in 'The Knight's Tale'. In *Boece*, Chaucer's own version of the *De Consolatione Philosophiae*, he translates:

> Thus, at the laste, it byhoveth the to suffren wyth evene wil in pacience al that is doon inwith the floor of Fortune (that is to seyn, in this world), syn thou hast oonys put thy nekke undir the yok of hir.
>
> (Book II, Prosa 1, 91 et seq.)

The emphasis is on man's behaviour 'in this world' and there is no suggestion either in Boethius or in Chaucer of the possibility of redemption in a life after death, although at the end of *Troilus and Criseyde*, where the characters are bound by the same Boethian principles, Chaucer seems to have had second thoughts when he inserted the palinode:

> O yonge, fresshe folkes, he or she,
> In which that love up groweth with youre age,
> Repeyreth hom fro worldly vanyte,
> And of youre herte up casteth the visage
> To thilke God that after his ymage
> Yow made, and thynketh al nys but a faire
> This world, that passeth soone as floures faire.
>
> (*Tr*, Book 5, 1835–41)

In 'The Knight's Tale' there is no such hint of any Christian doctrine: Arcite dies, and we are told,

> His spirit chaunged hous and wente ther,
> As I cam nevere, I kan nat tellen wher.
> Therfore I stynte, I nam no divinistre;
> Of soules fynde I nat in this registre,

Ne me ne list thilke opinions to telle
Of hem, though that they writen wher they dwelle.
Arcite is coold, ther Mars his soule gye!

(2809–15)

The irony is heightened in the abrupt dismissal and the hasty excuse in which Chaucer, the Christian poet, through the narrator, the Christian Knight, is denying responsibility for such views. Boethius is really more optimistic in tone than anything in 'The Knight's Tale', as can be seen from Chaucer's own translation in *Boece*:

> For yif thou therfore wenest thiself nat weleful, for thynges that tho semeden joyeful ben passed, ther nys nat why thow sholdest wene thiself a wrecche; for thynges that semen now sory passen also.
>
> (Book II, Prosa 3, 75 et seq.)

'The Knight's Tale' reflecting the pessimism of the Middle Ages, can only offer the exhortation,

> To maken vertu of necessitee,
> And take it weel that we may nat eschue,
> And namely that to us alle is due.
>
> (3042–4)

Chaucer's Knight, having his own precise place in the feudal hierarchy, with its concern for order in society, would, despite Theseus's lack of any overt Christianity, have had some fellow-feeling for the Duke, who is the character through whom all the philosophic pronouncements are made. 'Providence is the very Divine reason itself, seated in the highest Prince, which disposeth of all things,' says Boethius, and this is the Duke's own function in the Tale, disposing on earth by a kind of Divine Right, the authority of 'That same Prince and that Moevere', who

> Hath stablissed in this wrecched world adoun
> Certeyne dayes and duracioun. . . .
>
> (2995–6)

After the variety of the portraits in 'The General Prologue' it is, perhaps, surprising that the characters in the first Tale should be presented in such a formalized manner. Theseus himself is the only one to stand out as an individual and, as we have already seen, he is introduced at the outset as little more than an actor

in a stylised ritualistic drama, and the mouthpiece for the philosophical content of the poem. Nevertheless, as the Tale develops he emerges as a character who asserts his authority, but does so with restraint and humanity. It would, indeed, have been inappropriate to differentiate too obviously between Palamon and Arcite, for to have done so would have been to weaken the examination of the apparent inequality of the justice meted out by Providence, which is the theme of the Tale. As personalities, of course, there is some difference. The love which Palamon, who symbolises the whole conception of romantic Courtly Love, bears for Emily is on a more exalted plane than that of his rival, who symbolises the chivalric military code. In defending himself against Palamon's accusation of breaking their bond as sworn blood brothers Arcite says that

> '. . . Thou woost nat yet now
> Wheither she be a womman or goddesse!
> Thyn is affeccioun of hoolynesse,
> And myn is love, as to a creature . . .'
>
>   (1156–9)

and we are satisfied that each has an equal right to the lady's affections even if Palamon did see her first. When, through the intervention of Perotheus, Arcite is released from prison we sympathize with Palamon who is left behind in captivity, but before we are told of Palamon's distress at remaining behind, acknowledging defeat in the face of his adversary's greater advantages, Arcite has bewailed the fact that in his freedom he is worse off than he was before:

> Now is me shape eternally to dwelle.
> Noght in purgatorie, but in helle.
>
>   (1225–6)

When viewed objectively there is little to choose between the claims of the two lovers, but it is the difference in their temperaments that will determine our support for one rather than the other. Palamon appears to have the purer motives, is more of a visionary who worships Emily as a goddess, and goes to pray for her in the temple of Venus; Arcite is more the worldly man of action, showing much greater initiative during his freedom by organizing his return in disguise to Theseus's court to be near Emily, and he is the warrior who prays to Mars for victory.

The characters of these two young men are presented in the same kind of two-dimensional form as the characters in a Kafka novel where there is the same preoccupation with a sense of justice as imposed by a bureaucratic government. Kafka's novels have been interpreted as prophetic political allegories foretelling the plight of central European Jewry in the mid-twentieth century. It is tempting to view 'The Knight's Tale' in a similar way as anticipating by some seven or eight years the tragic events which marked the close of Richard II's reign, with the contrasted personalities of the cousins Palamon and Arcite representing the conflict between the visionary, self-indulgent king and his politically ambitious, military-minded cousin, Henry Bolingbroke. The closing events of this reign, too, were determined by the settlement of the argument between two disputant knights in a trial by arms arranged by the highest authority in the land, which then banished them as Arcite was banished by Duke Theseus. Further point is given to the satire when one realizes that the red and white of Theseus's banner are also King Richard's own livery colours. There could also be some double-edged irony in the fact that, although Arcite is victorious in the feat of arms, it brings him little lasting earthly reward.

To say that 'The Knight's Tale' is deficient in the subtle delineation of the characters as complex individuals, is not to deny the Tale considerable narrative force. Chaucer tells us that it was universally popular among the pilgrims themselves, appealing especially to the 'gentils' in the company. For the modern reader some 'willing suspension of disbelief' is necessary, but we need not, as has been suggested, give ourselves over entirely to the world of faery and romance to offset the apparent lack of characterization and probability of action. A triangular love contest is as popular as ever it was, and the lack of characterization does not diminish the interest. We are just as curious to know who is going to win in the end, and the delaying of the action by the colourful build-up to the big fight creates considerable suspense.

If the theme of the Tale is to wrestle with an abstract problem of philosophy, the philosopher and the poet realize that the problem has to be resolved 'in this world' so the story itself is set against the most concrete of backgrounds described in some of the most forceful poetry in the language. The authentic world of medieval tourney is described with the arrival of Lycurgus and

Emetrius, the two knights in attendance on Palamon and Arcite respectively. These are two more symbolic figures representing the pomp and power of majesty, but Chaucer does not deny them their own peculiar physical characteristics. Of Lycurgus he says:

> Blak was his berd, and manly was his face;
> The cercles of his eyen in his heed,
> They gloweden bitwixen yelow and reed,
> And lik a grifphon looked he aboute,
> With kempe heeris on his browes stoute;
> His lymes grete, his brawnes harde and stronge,
> His shuldres brode, his armes rounde and longe . . .
>
> (2130–6)

And of Emetrius:

> His crispe heer lyk rynges was yronne,
> And that was yelow, and glytered as the sonne.
> His nose was heigh, his eyen bright citryn,
> His lippes rounde, his colour was sangwyn;
> A fewe frakenes in his face yspreynd,
> Bitwixen yelow and somdel blak ymeynd;
> And as a leon he his lookyng caste.
>
> (2165–71)

The world of romance may be emphasized by the comparison with the heraldic gryphon and lion, but the other physical details such as the coarse facial hairs and glowing eyes of the one and the freckles of the other are as acute and realistic as anything in 'The General Prologue', while the reference to the colours would have especial significance to a medieval audience. Nor does the symbolical function of the other characters cause Chaucer to disregard entirely physical differences: Palamon is distinguished by his 'flotery berd and ruggy, asshy heeres', Arcite is 'long and big of bones' and Emily has her yard-long golden tresses crowned with a garland of flowers. Realism abounds in the graphic detailed descriptions of the pre-tournament preparations:

> Nailynge the speres, and helmes bokelynge;
> Giggynge of sheeldes, with layneres lacynge
> (There as nede is they weren no thyng ydel);
> The fomy steedes on the golden brydel
> Gnawynge, and faste the armurers also

With fyle and hamer prikynge to and fro. . . .

(2503-8)

This is as authentic and realistic as Shakespeare's account in *Henry V* of the preparations in the English camp before the battle of Agincourt:

> . . . and from the tents
> The armourers, accomplishing the knights,
> With busy hammers closing rivets up,
> Give dreadful note of preparation.

The Athenian tournament is vividly described:

> In goon the speres ful sadly in arrest;
> In gooth the sharpe spore into the syde.
> Ther seen men who kan juste and who kan ryde;
> Ther shyveren shaftes upon sheeldes thikke;
> He feeleth thurgh the herte-spoon the prikke.
> Up spryngen speres twenty foot on highte;
> Out goon the swerdes as the silver brighte;
> The helmes they tohewen and toshrede;
> Out brest the blood with stierne stremes rede;
> With myghty maces the bones they tobreste.

(2602-11)

Here the bold alliterative verse with its Anglo-Saxon vocabulary and the emphatically strong verbs and end-stopped lines conveys all the ferocity of the conflict which is perfectly suited to the epic and heroic atmosphere of the Tale.

The sudden and unexpected reversal of fortune at the height of Arcite's success is dismissed rapidly, but the tension mounts with the minutiae of the medical details of his fatal injury. The same extravagance is expended on Arcite's funeral preparations as were lavished during his life, and his corpse is bedecked with cloth of gold.

These lengthy descriptions themselves, together with the long speeches of Theseus, have been considered by some as contributing to the apparent lack of verisimilitude in the Tale. It should, however, be clear from the language that the poet is realistically depicting the virile, masculine medieval world in which he lived; but, in order to accord with his ironic treatment of Boethian ideas, emphasizing the stress his contemporaries laid upon worldly externals and neglecting to some extent the

importance they also attached to spiritual values. The pronouncements of Theseus do tend to slow up the tempo of the
poem at times, seldom carrying the action any further forward,
but a slow majestic pace is not inappropriate to the dignified
theme of the Tale and is in keeping, not only with the character
of Theseus, but also with the Knight himself whom we can
imagine as being slow and ponderous at times, yet terse at others,
and particularly exuberant when recounting any military exploits. In any case, although the elevated tone is maintained
throughout the Tale, it is relieved by some colloquial touches and
homely dialogue. The rhetorical device of *occupatio* is used to
proceed to the next development of the story because 'shortly
for to telle is myn entente', or even more chattily down to earth,
and this surprisingly in the formal opening to the Tale:

> But al that thyng I moot as now forbere.
> I have, God woot, a large feeld to ere,
> And wayke been the oxen in my plough.
>
> (885–7)

There is the easy conversational style of the tit-for-tat finality of
Arcite's

> 'Thow shalt', quod he, 'be rather fals than I;
> And thou art fals, I telle thee outrely,
> For paramour I loved hire first er thow.
> What wiltow seyen?'
>
> (1153–6)

Even in a philosophical passage Arcite says, 'We faren as he that
dronke is as a mous' (1261), a simile which is also used by the
worldly Wife of Bath. Theseus himself can be almost flippant at
times, as when he describes the irrational behaviour of the lovers
and says of the object of their affections that,

> 'She woot namoore of al this hoote fare,
> By God, than woot a cokkow or an hare!
> But all moot ben assayed, hoot and coold;
> A man moot ben a fool, or yong or oold. . . .'
>
> (1809–12)

The great sense of excitement in Athens is conveyed not only
by the graphic descriptions of the tournament, but also by the
enthusiastic comments of the supporters in the Athenian crowd
as they take sides and extol the virtues of their champions:

Somme seyden thus, somme seyde 'it shal be so';
Somme helden with hym with the blake berd,
Somme with the balled, somme with the thikke herd;
Somme seyde he looked grymme, and he wolde fighte;
'He hath a sparth of twenty pound of wighte.'

(2516–20)

A striking feature of this Tale is the degree of unity and balance in its structure.[2] The arrangement of all the characters in the Tale is perfectly balanced. The two earthly knights of identical status, who strive for the love of the same lady, are paralleled in the supernatural world by Venus (Palamon), Mars (Arcite) and Diana (Emily), and are presided over by Saturn, who performs the same judicial role on this plane as Theseus on earth. While over them all,

'Thanne may men by this ordre wel discerne
That thilke Moevere stable is and eterne.'

(3003–4)

This sense of order and stability is conveyed throughout by Duke Theseus. He redresses the balance by avenging the deaths of the Theban husbands, he resolves the quarrel between the two lovers by elevating the scene from a backwoods brawl to one with all the magnificent pomp and splendour of a royal tournament within the rigid rules of courtly conduct, and he unites Palamon and Emily in Christian marriage with all due decorum. The lists, which he orders to be built, are circular in shape and there is complete uniformity in the arrangement of the altars and the temples, each of which is described in the same logical way; Lycurgus and his retinue of exactly one hundred knights balances that of Emetrius and his equal number of followers, and the whole procedure adopted by the contestants before the tournament is identical. In the funeral procession old Egeus balances Theseus. The precise numerical details all help to stress the concern for regularity: 'And this day fifty wykes, fer ne ner', 'The circuit a myle was aboute', 'Ful of degrees, the heighte of sixty pas'. In the first instance the lists are erected on the site of the original disorganized duel and it is on the same spot that Arcite's sepulchre is built. This enormous emphasis on the structural unity of the Tale helps to cloak some of the ambivalence in the philosophical doctrine behind the story itself

with its overriding belief that man is subject to all the irrational
whimsicalities of Dame Fortune and the more rational approach
of Theseus as expressed in the lines,

> '. . . Right so ther lyved never man,' he seyde,
> 'In al this world, that som tyme he ne deyde.
> This world nys but a thurghfare ful of wo,
> And we been pilgrymes, passynge to and fro.'
> (2845–8)

It is Theseus who maintains the courtly ideals of chivalric order
in the face of all the forces of disorder.

These forces of disorder are represented in the Tale by the
conflict between the two lovers. This conflict is a twofold one:
there is the love conflict, but there is also the conflict of loyalty
between the two young men; a loyalty of kinship since they were
cousins, and a loyalty of friendship as sworn brothers, and also
each was 'ybounden as a knyght' to the other. Loyalty was, of
course, at the heart of the feudal system, but here again Chaucer
mirrors his more immediate courtly circle with its many romantic
attachments between king and courtier.[3] It is one of the conventions of the Courtly Love code that lovers refer to each other in
terms of friendship while the loyalty between friends is often
expressed in the more passionate language of love. In 'The
Franklin's Tale' we are told,

> That freendes everych oother moot obeye,
> If they wol longe holden compaignye.
> Love wol nat been constreyned by maistrye.
> (762–4)

And in the same Tale the whole relationship between Arveragus
and Dorigen after their marriage is conveyed in the more un-
emotional and practical language of a contract between friends:

> Thus hath she take hir servant and hir lord,—
> Servant in love, and lord in mariage.
> Thanne was he bothe in lordshipe and servage.
> (792–4)

Whereas there were no similar ties of loyalty between Arveragus
and Aurelius as there were between Palamon and Arcite, nevertheless Arveragus, when he hears of Dorigen's dilemma, insists
that she honours her contract for 'Trouthe is the hyeste thyng

that man may kepe', and it is Aurelius who releases her because
he sees her husband's 'grete gentillesse'. This emphasis on the
importance of the loyalty of friendship was carried to the highest
level by St Thomas Aquinas who used it to express the relationship between God and man; and in support of this concept were
resurrected all the 'old ideas of divine friendship, the sources of
which could be found in Stoicism and Boethius'.[4]

Of all the *Canterbury Tales* this opening story which super-
ficially appears to be a straightforward conventional medieval
romance within the framework of contemporary thought, is one
of the most difficult to evaluate. It is, with certain reservations,
an appealing short story, but with all its spectacular settings it is
clearly no mere glittering pageant of courtly life in the Middle
Ages. Like a great Gothic cathedral with its pinnacled spires
reaching skywards into the unknown, it reflects the medieval preoccupation with the great questions of human existence. As
Charles Muscatine says: 'The impressive, patterned edifice of the
noble life, its dignity and richness, its regard for law and decorum, are all bulwarks against the ever-threatening forces of
chaos, and in constant collision with them.'[5] Writing in an age
so concerned with degree and the order of Nature, Chaucer has
infused Boccaccio's story with the concepts of Boethian philosophy in order to discuss the universal problem of man's en-
durance in the face of circumstances that are beyond his control.
Human beings caught up in the great political issues of the
twentieth century are presented with the same heart-searching
doubts and may be tempted to echo Gloucester's

> As flies to wanton boys are we to th'gods;
> They kill us for their sport

unless they believe with Edgar that 'the gods are just' and that

> Men must endure
> Their going hence, even as their coming hither:
> Ripeness is all.

This is the Stoic wisdom that 'The Knight's Tale' teaches by
encouraging us 'to maken vertu of necessitee' for,

> ... certeinly a man hath moost honour
> To dyen in his excellence and flour ...
> (3047–8)

The Tales of the Prioress and the Clerk

'Be preue & be pacient, in payne & in joye,
For he þat is to rakel to renden his cloþeʒ,
Mot efte sitte wyth more vn-sounde to sewe hem togeder.'
For-þy when pouerte me enpreceʒ & payneʒ in-noʒe,
Ful softly wyth suffraunce saʒttel me bihoue,
For þe penaunce & payne to preue hit in syʒt,—
Þat pacience is a nobel poynt, þaʒ hit displese ofte.
(*Patience*: lines 525–31)[1]

In Rochester Cathedral there is a sculpture which represents with striking directness the attitude to the Jews which was prevalent in the thirteenth century.[2] The carved figure holds in one hand the Tables of the Law, the traditional basis of Jewish teaching. In the other hand is a broken staff, symbolic of the broken authority of the Synagogue. And the figure is blindfolded, in accordance with the view that blind ignorance and stubborn folly was the cause of the Jewish refusal to accept Christian teaching. This attitude to the Jews and their faith was not confined to England,[3] but could be found throughout Europe, and it resulted in widespread persecution of Jewish communities during the thirteenth century.

The religious beliefs of the Jews and the fervour with which they adhered to their faith led to fear and misunderstanding on the part of the majority of common folk. This fear was not, however, based on religious grounds alone. The Jews became identified with the many social disasters which frequently disrupted medieval life, and the ignorant attributed such hardships as famine and plague to the magical scheming of Jewish conspiracies. It is not difficult to imagine how such ideas arose. It was the custom for Jews to live in small tribal communities, and superstitious minds readily imagined that they were indulging in activities hostile to Christendom within the secret depths of these ghettos. Only the uneducated, however, subscribed to such beliefs. More important than their superstitions were the attitudes of the higher classes.

During the earlier centuries of the Middle Ages the Jews enjoyed a favourable social position. They were skilled in financial affairs, and, most important, they used coinage rather than the simple exchange of goods in their trading. Such operations were forbidden to Christians, who were prohibited from activities like money-lending on the grounds that Christ condemned such men when he expelled the usurers and merchants from the temple in Jerusalem. So the Jews provided an essential service as financiers, and for this reason they came under the protection of certain kings (most notably Charlemagne and William the

Conqueror). This protection brought with it binding restrictions: 'The Jew can have nothing that is his own, for whatever he acquires, he acquires, not for himself, but for the king; for the Jews live not for themselves but for others.'[4] But although the Jew belonged to the king as a piece of property, he was the equal of all other subjects of the king, and, in addition, he enjoyed special privileges. This situation created envy and hostility towards the Jews, and aggravated religious opposition by adding to it social motives.

The Jews' privileged position was undermined by the rise of the merchants. As soon as Christians were permitted to loan on usury, the Jewish contribution to medieval economic affairs became less important. They began to face competition, and the new merchants, for their part, gained in power by combining their forces against their rivals and forming gilds. The merchants were helped by a number of restrictions imposed on the Jews (for example, in 1271 they were forbidden to hold land). As their social position became weaker, propaganda increased against them. They were accused of extreme wickedness, and during the second half of the thirteenth century we witness a campaign, vigorously supported by certain sections of the Church, which displays all the hatred and fear which had, to a large extent, remained hidden during the years of royal protection. This campaign roused many to violence against the Jewish ghettos in their towns, and there are records of massacres of Jews in Bishop's Lynn (now King's Lynn), Stamford and Lincoln. The Jews were driven to retaliation. Then in 1290, Edward I, with typical ruthlessness, expelled all Jews from England.

Much of Chaucer's 'Prioress's Tale' belongs to the thirteenth century, and his story of ritual murder has a close connection with the violent campaign of propaganda which was conducted against the Jews as their power declined. The most obvious parallel to his Tale is the legend of St Hugh of Lincoln, who was murdered by Jews in 1255. Chaucer recalls this story at the conclusion of the Tale:

> O yonge Hugh of Lyncoln, slayn also
> With cursed Jewes, as it is notable
> For it is but a litel while ago,
> Preye eek for us . . .
>
> (684–7)

It is significant that, although Chaucer is writing more than a century after the martyrdom of St Hugh, he expects his readers to recall the event readily. The story was clearly a popular one, and one which played an important part in the anti-Jewish movement. The Tale told by the Prioress would have been similarly well known, though not, perhaps, in exactly the form presented by Chaucer. He accepts in his version the basic facts of a traditional story without major qualification, and the use he makes of common ideas of Jewish tribalism and evil can only be understood in the light of the social and economic events of the thirteenth century.

Although the part played by the Jews in the Tale is a key one, it is not the main focus of Chaucer's imagination. The Tale is, in one sense, about violence, but it is not a violent tale. Its style has nothing of the vigorous energy of parts of 'The Canon's Yeoman's Tale', and certainly it is far removed from the compelling violence of rhythm and language in 'The Pardoner's Tale':

> This cursed man hath in his hond yhent
> This poysoun in a box, and sith he ran
> Into the nexte strete unto a man,
> And borwed of hym large botelles thre;
> And in the two his poyson poured he;
> The thridde he kepte clene for his drynke.
> For al the nyght he shoop hym for to swynke
> In cariynge of the gold out of that place.
> And whan this riotour, with sory grace,
> Hadde filled with wyn his grete botels thre,
> To his felawes agayn repaireth he.
>
> (868–78)

'The Prioress's Tale' is about murder, but Chaucer is more interested in the human suffering and religious symbolism of the events than in the details of the crime itself.

Religious symbolism of the kind used in this Tale would have been very familiar to Chaucer's contemporaries. During the fourteenth and fifteenth centuries there appeared numerous collections of Saints Legends, and Chaucer's Tale belongs to this genre. It may be that he found the basic material for 'The Prioress's Tale' in such a collection, and he certainly reproduces in his short poem their style and tone. Some of these legends set out to extol the virtues of the Blessed Virgin, and this is the

purpose of the Tale with which the Prioress entertains the pilgrims: it is a Miracle of the Virgin. Although the Tale is based on superstition, we know that common folk in the Middle Ages would have accepted it easily. They were encouraged to do so by the Church, which readily used the imaginations of the uneducated for the furtherance of its own teaching. Superstition was an important aspect of religious experience, and many of the stories, or *exempla*, told by the Church to illustrate its theological and moral ideas were based on the connection between superstition and religion. Ideas which would have remained incomprehensible to ordinary people gained striking immediacy in this way, and Saints Legends played an essential part in the Church's work.

The Prologue to 'The Prioress's Tale' takes the form of an Invocation to Christ and, more especially, to the Virgin Mary. The inclusion of an invocation of this kind was a common literary convention in the genre of Miracles and Saints Legends. Chaucer follows the traditional form closely, although he uses his invocation not simply as a formal device, but as a means of telling us a great deal about the speaker and the subject of her Tale. The Tale itself is of a child, and it is significant that the Prioress refers twice to children in her Prologue:

> But by the mouth of children thy bountee
> Parfourned is, for on the brest soukynge
> Somtyme shewen they thyn heriynge . . .
> But as a child of twelf month oold, or lesse,
> That kan unnethes any word expresse,
> Right so fare I . . .
>
> (457–9, 484–6)

These phrases provide an important link with the subsequent narrative, and they also invite us to recall the picture of gentle sentimentality which characterizes the Prioress in 'The General Prologue':

> But, for to speken of hire conscience,
> She was so charitable and so pitous
> She wolde wepe, if that she saugh a mous
> Kaught in a trappe, if it were deed or bledde . . .
> And al was conscience and tendre herte.
>
> (142–5, 150)

It is also appropriate to her ecclesiastical office that the Prioress should employ the language and imagery of the Bible and the Services of the Church. Since the Tale is a Miracle of the Virgin, much of the Prologue establishes an important connection with the Virgin Mary. Chaucer employs two common traditional symbols of the Virgin, the 'white lylye flour' and the 'bussh unbrent', and he also refers closely to passages in the Office of the Blessed Virgin. The opening stanza of the Prologue, for example, is a paraphrase of the first two verses of Psalm 8, with which the service of Matins in the Office of the Blessed Virgin commences. Throughout the Prologue Chaucer uses religious material in this way, and thus he creates the atmosphere of piety and innocence around which the Tale is constructed.

Some scholars have noted other religious echoes in the Prologue. The most notable of these is the interesting argument of Marie Hamilton[5] which suggests that Chaucer quotes from or refers to much of the Mass for the Feast of the Holy Innocents (The Feast of Childermas). During the late Middle Ages this was a popular Church festival in which children took a major part. It was the custom for a boy bishop to be chosen who would lead the other choirboys or schoolboys in the ceremonies. The festival focused attention on the arrival of children at the gateway to maturity, and this would be symbolized by the leadership of the boy bishop, who 'in various places in England . . . as part of his assumption of mature responsibility, preached a sermon at Mass.'[6] The 'litel clergeon' of 'The Prioress's Tale' is younger than those who would play a large part in the Childermas ceremonies, but it may be that he is representative of childhood itself since Chaucer states that he is 'seven yeer of age', the age at which, according to medieval ideas, the seven-year period of childhood began.

The three opening stanzas of the narrative characterize the perfect form of the Tale as a whole. Chaucer begins with a generalized location, and then slowly narrows his focus through a decreasing vista onto the child with whom the Tale is concerned. He employs this same technique with equal effect in other tales (for example, that of the Clerk). It is clear that Chaucer desires a more specific setting than is initially suggested by the phrases 'in Asye, in a greet citee', and in only a few lines he presents a closely visualized description of the streets and

buildings where his story takes place. Since the Jews were expelled from England nearly a century before Chaucer wrote his
Tale, it was necessary for him to set the narrative in some remote area. But although we are told that the story takes place in
Asia (and this setting seems to be Chaucer's own invention),
there is much which suggests that he has in mind a much more
immediate location. The street which he describes seems very
familiar to him:

> And thurgh the strete men myghte ride or wende,
> For it was free and open at eyther ende.

(493–4)

So does the school, which 'stood / Doun at the ferther ende'.
Perhaps Chaucer has in mind an actual Jewish quarter, such as
the one at Norwich which he might well have seen, although it
would no longer have been occupied by Jews. The Norwich
colony enjoyed royal protection of the kind described earlier in
this chapter, and this position would have been remarkably
similar to that which the Prioress condemns so vigorously in the
opening stanza of her Tale:

> Ther was in Asye, in a greet citee,
> Amonges Cristene folk, a Jewerye,
> Sustened by a lord of that contree
> For foule usure and lucre of vileynye,
> Hateful to Crist and to his compaignye . . .

(488–92)

The brief description of the school is similarly realistic: it has all
the noise and bustle of a crowd of children. It is unlikely that
these are choirboys, and the 'litel clergeon' is a boy at the com-
mencement of his ordinary schooling. He does not belong to the
group who 'lerned hire antiphoner'.

Chaucer's introduction of the 'litel clergeon' has the same kind of
realism that we find in the details of the location of the narrative.
The boy's activities at school and his relationship with his widowed
mother are described in simple, direct language. Chaucer's details
are few, but they are carefully selected. The realism of the narrative is increased by the introduction of the older schoolboy, a
character who does not occur in any earlier versions of the story.
The tone of the 'felawe's' reply to the 'litel clergeon's' question
about the *Alma redemptoris* is short and to the point:

His felawe, which that elder was than he,
Answerde hym thus: 'This song, I have herd seye,
Was maked of our blisful Lady free,
Hire to salue, and eek hire for to preye
To been oure help and socour whan we deye.
I kan namoore expounde in this mateere;
I lerne song, I kan but smal grammeere.'

(530–6)

The last two lines in particular seem entirely suited to his character.

It can be seen that much of Chaucer's description during the first few stanzas of the narrative is realistic, but there are other associations which he develops, and which make an important contribution to the symbolic aspect of the Tale. Chaucer is concerned to exemplify an ideal, the ideal of innocence, which is represented by the 'litel clergeon'. His choice of the age of seven for the child (he is older in other versions of the story) emphasizes this sense of innocence, as does the appropriate reference to the boy saint, Nicholas, of whom the Prioress says:

But ay, whan I remembre on this mateere,
Seint Nicholas stant evere in my presence,
For he so yong to Crist dide reverence.

(513–15)

The same sense of innocence is present in the child's eager questioning of the older boy, and in the determination with which he learns and sings the *Alma redemptoris*. He sings this hymn to the praise of the Virgin Mary, just as the Prioress dedicated her Tale to the Blessed Virgin in her Prologue. The connection here is not accidental, and Chaucer is at pains to sustain the link by the insistent repetition of the word 'Crist', which occurs seven times in the first four stanzas of the Tale, and, more important, in the words spoken by the 'litel clergeon' himself: 'I wol it konne Oure Lady for to honoure!' So important is this idea that Chaucer breaks off his narrative and includes a whole stanza about the child's offering to the Virgin Mary:

As I have seyd, thurghout the Juerie,
This litel child, as he cam to and fro,
Ful murily than wolde he synge and crie
O Alma redemptoris everemo.

> The swetnesse hath his herte perced so
> Of Cristes mooder that, to hire to preye,
> He kan nat stynte of syngyng by the weye.
>
> (551-7)

This stanza is also an important factor in the dramatic structure of the Tale. The pause which Chaucer creates at this point emphasizes the picture of innocence which he has built up, and this then contrasts most strikingly with the scheming cruelty of the Jews which becomes apparent when the narrative continues. This deliberate juxtaposition of opposites is an important feature of the Tale, and the skill with which Chaucer handles it contributes much to the success of the whole poem.

When the events of the narrative are resumed, Chaucer again uses direct speech. This gives added drama and realism since the speech is used to illustrate the thoughts in the minds of the Jews. Chaucer externalizes their psychology by giving the tempting words to Satan, and he also establishes a link between the Jews and the Devil, an idea exactly in accordance with the traditional thirteenth-century attitude to the Jews. What is more, this device also suggests a direct link between the child victim and Christ. Another interesting detail is the hiring of the killer. This serves to add realism and character interest, and it is appropriate in view of the common idea that Jews used their wealth in the pursuit of evil.

During the account of the activities of these Jews the verse moves rapidly, and the language is swift and direct. The murder of the 'litel clergeon' is accomplished in the short space of three lines:

> And as the child gan forby for to pace,
> This cursed Jew hym hente, and heeld hym faste,
> And kitte his throte, and in a pit hym caste.
>
> (569-71)

This recalls the climax of 'The Pardoner's Tale', which is concluded with similar speed. The brevity of the account in 'The Prioress's Tale' shows that Chaucer is not so much concerned with the crime itself as with the motives behind it and, more important, with the consequences which ensue. The final contrast with the purity and innocence of the murdered child comes with the casting of the body into the foul pit. The detail

is dramatic and realistic, but it also suggests a symbolic association in the idea that the purity of the child is defiled by the action of the Jews.

The two stanzas which follow the murder of the child serve two functions. There is, first, the use of rhetorical devices which Chaucer frequently employs at the climax of his Tales. He appeals to the emotions of his audience with two *exclamationes*:

> O cursed folk of Herodes al newe,
> What may youre yvel entente yow availle? . . .
> O martir, sowded to virginitee,
> Now maystow syngen . . .
>
> (574–5, 579–80)

In this passage, Chaucer also commands his listeners' thoughts in a rhetorical question. And there is a third device which he uses, that of the proverb, or *sententia*: 'Mordre wol out, certeyn, it wol nat faille' (576). The heightened emotional response produced by such rhetorical figures is not, however, the only feature of these stanzas. Chaucer is also concerned to emphasize the symbolic quality of the death of the child. The Prioress intends us to look upon the child as a martyr and the remainder of the Tale supports this. The reference to Herod and the use of the word 'innocent' (line 566) invite us to recall an earlier occasion when innocent children were murdered by Jews, the Massacre of the Innocents. In addition, these stanzas state the traditional belief in the Book of Revelation that children who died a martyr's death like the Holy Innocents would join the chosen in heaven who praise the 'white Lamb celestial':

> O martir, sowded to virginitee,
> Now maystow syngen, folwynge evere in oon
> The white Lamb celestial—quod she—
> Of which the grete evaungelist, Seint John,
> In Pathmos wroot, which seith that they that goon
> Biforn this Lamb, and synge a song al newe,
> That nevere, flesshly, wommen they ne knewe.
>
> (579–85)

In these lines the syntax is disjointed and the rhythm of the verse becomes markedly slower. In this way Chaucer shows that one section of the Tale is at an end, and the Prioress gives a dramatic pause before she returns to the situation of the widow. There is

a marked contrast between the simple and direct language which Chaucer uses to describe the poignant fear of the widow, and the rich symbolism of the description of the singing of the dead child:

> O grete God, that parfournest thy laude
> By mouth of innocentz, lo, heere thy myght!
> This gemme of chastite, this emeraude,
> And eek of martirdom the ruby bright,
> Ther he with throte ykorven lay upright,
> He *Alma redemptoris* gan to synge
> So loude that al the place gan to rynge.
>
> (607–13)

The images of the precious stones are common in religious poetry of the Middle Ages, but though they are conventional they are none the less appropriate. The red of the ruby reminds us of the blood of the boy and of Christ, and the images may also anticipate the 'greyn' on the boy's tongue, which is probably a pearl.

From this point in the Tale to its conclusion realism and idealization alternate. Chaucer returns to dramatic realism in the account of the summoning of the Provost and the procession to the abbey. The punishment of the Jews, in particular, is presented with striking directness, and the inclusion of a simple proverb helps to produce this matter-of-fact tone:

> 'Yvele shal have that yvele wol deserve';
> Therfore with wilde hors he dide hem drawe,
> And after that he heng hem by the lawe.
>
> (632–4)

The same realism is present in the implied criticism of contemporary corruption in the Church which Chaucer includes in his description of the abbot:

> This abbot, which that was an hooly man,
> As monkes been—or elles oghte be—
>
> (642–3)

Parts of the dialogue between the abbot and the child which ensues also have a kind of realism, but we are aware of an added perspective here, one of deep pathos which goes beyond the simple facts. This is particularly true of the last stanza spoken by the child:

'Wherfore I synge, and synge moot certeyn,
In honour of that blisful Mayden free,
Til fro my tonge of taken is the greyn;
And after that thus seyde she to me:
"My litel child, now wol I fecche thee,
Whan that the greyn is fro thy tonge ytake.
Be nat agast, I wol thee nat forsake."'

(663–9)

The vocabulary continues to be straightforward, and the rhythm
and tone carefully controlled. There is no hint of melodrama.
Rather the effect is of real pathos, just as it is in the account of
the mother's swoon, where Chaucer avoids excess (something
which he fails to do in a similar section in 'The Clerk's Tale') in
a brief and disciplined narrative.

Closely linked with this heightened effect are the symbolic
associations which continue to play an important part. The
parallel of the mother with Rachel serves both to intensify her
human plight and emotions, and also to elevate her situation to a
significance beyond the human. We are reminded again of the
symbolic association of the mother with the Virgin Mary, and of
the identification of the 'litel clergeon' with other martyrs like
St Hugh of Lincoln and the Holy Innocents. Finally, the last
words of the child and the concluding stanzas of the Tale recall
the theme of praise to the Virgin Mary, which is the Prioress's
main purpose. Just as the Tale began with an invocation to the
Blessed Virgin, so, as it draws quietly to a close with the slower
rhythms of the long French syllables ('unstable', 'merciable' and
'multiplie'), it is concluded with a conventional benediction
which appeals to the grace of the Virgin.

This is a short Tale where much is achieved in a little space.
The main success of the narrative stems from the skilful alternation between realism and idealism. The pathos of the Tale is
created through the relationship of the boy and his mother. On
the human level, this relationship is an idealistic one, but the
Tale does not descend to melodrama because Chaucer never loses
sight of the realities of the story, the closely recorded details of
the town and school, the older schoolboy, and the conversations
which take place in the Tale. On the spiritual level, too, the boy
represents an ideal of innocence and purity, and this is intensified because it is never expressed abstractly or with excess,

but always through the realistic details of the story. We have
seen how this alternation of meaning is reflected in the style of
the Tale, which varies from the detailed realism of the opening
stanza to the mystical symbolism of the description of the
miracle of the singing. Both aspects of the style are important,
but the combination of them produces a Tale which is not,
primarily, a realistic one. Its effect is clearly very different from
that of 'The Nun's Priest's Tale' or parts of 'The Pardoner's
Tale'.

'The Prioress's Tale' has much in common with the great
medieval poem *Pearl*,[7] though it lacks its philosophic dimension.
In both the main purpose is the celebration of an ideal of innocent purity. The style which Chaucer has chosen is often childlike in its simplicity. The vocabulary and imagery is based on
simple everyday life, and the rhythms of the verse are gentle.
There is often much repetition of phrases and words, and
much of the vocabulary is childlike in tone:

> This *litel* child, as he cam *to and fro*,
> Ful *murily* than wolde he synge and crie . . .
>
> (552–3)

The characters of the story are plain and briefly drawn, and their
emotions are correspondingly simple and straightforward. And
the background of the story is drawn in a similar way. Realism
is not excluded, but it is simplified and subordinated to serve a
wider purpose.

'The Clerk's Tale' is in many ways similar to that of the
Prioress, for its purpose is the celebration of another ideal—
patience. There are, however, a number of difficulties which face
the reader in an assessment of 'The Clerk's Tale' which are not
present in the story of the 'litel clergeon'. In the Tale of Griselda
the moral positives seem to be confused, and there appears to be
a lack of real motive and purpose in the actions and thoughts of
the characters. The style, too, presents problems. It does not,
for the most part, delight the reader with the usual vigour and
colour of Chaucer's later verse, but rather it seems flat and un-
inspired, and at times melodramatic and repetitive. Yet we should
not expect all Chaucer's Tales to be like that of the Nun's Priest.

'The Clerk's Tale' is an early work, and one which offers something quite different from the closely observed realism of human behaviour which we more readily associate with Chaucer's later art. It is this different conception which poses such problems for the modern reader, for 'The Clerk's Tale' belongs to a world very different from our own. Most of the values which it presupposes are quite foreign to us, and it is essential to come to terms with this background if any of the Tale's remarkable qualities are to be appreciated.

For the modern reader, the most problematic feature of the Tale is the suffering to which Griselda is subjected at the hands of her husband. It is clear, however, that Chaucer's contemporaries would have accepted Griselda's experience much more readily, because there is much in the Tale which closely corresponds to the actual condition and treatment of women in the Middle Ages. The medieval attitude to women may be largely attributed to St Paul, who looked upon them as a dangerous temptation to man. This view was expanded and emphasized by St Augustine and the early Fathers of the Church, of whom St Jerome represented the most striking condemnation of women: '. . . woman is the gate of the devil, the path of wickedness, the sting of the serpent, in a word a perilous object'.[8] This moral attitude influenced the legal position of women in the Middle Ages. They lacked many legal rights (most notably the right to succeed to a land inheritance), and in marriage they were looked upon as servants whose main task was to perform certain duties. This idea of female subservience allowed the husband to use violence against his wife, and many women suffered as a result from the harsh cruelty of men.[9]

Some women broke out of this restrictive scheme, and established for themselves positions of authority and influence. Such were the great political figures of the twelfth and thirteenth centuries like Blanche of Castile and Eleanor of Aquitaine. There were some, too, like Chaucer's Wife of Bath who contributed greatly to the economic life of the Middle Ages. And there were other women, like Agnes Paston,[10] who stood above their contemporaries by virtue of their great character and dignity. These, however, were a minority. It would seem that the experience of most married women was closer to that of the servant Griselda than the masterly Wife of Bath.

One important medieval movement may be seen as an attempt to change this prevailing situation and establish the supremacy of women over men. This movement, which we know as *Amour Courtois*, or Courtly Love, was an attempt to reverse the social rules and values of the court. Its bible, a treatise called *De Arte Honeste Amandi*, was written by Andreas Capellanus at the command of a great champion of feminine rights, Marie, Countess of Champagne. Marie de Champagne attacked marriage on the grounds that its duties were incompatible with love, and in doing so, she attacked God and the traditional values on which marriage was based. What Marie de Champagne attempted to break away from is, in fact, exactly what Griselda and Walter represent in an extreme form. And the ultimate effect of 'The Clerk's Tale' is to refute Andreas Capellanus and the whole Courtly Love tradition, and to re-state in a dramatic form the validity of the old ideals of duty and service which are justified by Griselda's experience.

In one sense, 'The Clerk's Tale' is an argument about love and marriage. This is an important aspect of the Tale because it forms part of the Marriage Debate which Chaucer conducts through a number of the *Canterbury Tales*. Within the Marriage Group, it functions as a reply to the Wife of Bath's attack on marriage, and this, to some extent, accounts for the Clerk's apparent exaggerations. It does not, however, represent Chaucer's answer; that task is performed by the Franklin. But it plays a key role in the progress towards a solution.

Like 'The Prioress's Tale', however, 'The Clerk's Tale' does not work on one level alone. It contains much more than a description of a marriage, or even an argument about duty and service in marriage. The Tale of Griselda has, in addition, many of the qualities of a Saint's Legend. It is not primarily a realistic Tale, but a story in which the characters and their actions are greatly simplified and given symbolic importance. The Tale uses a human relationship to illustrate spiritual truth in a way which was very common in the Middle Ages. It contains the same kind of juxtaposition which we find in some of the religious drama of the time (for example, the episode of Mak the Sheep-Stealer in the Second Towneley *Shepherds' Play*); and the incorporation of secular sentiment is a common feature of religious lyrics:

> When y se blosmes springe
>   ant here foules song,
> a suete loue-longynge
>   myn herte þourhout stong,
> al for a loue newe,
>   þat is so suete ant trewe,
>   þat gladieþ al my song;
> ich wot al myd iwisse
> my ioie ant eke my blisse
> on him is al ylong.[11]

The religious symbolism is the most important feature of the
Tale. Petrarch, in his version of the story, invested the narrative
with a religious purpose, and this Chaucer openly accepts:

> This storie is seyd, nat for that wyves sholde
> Folwen Grisilde as in humylitee,
> For it were inportable, though they wolde;
> But for that every wight, in his degree,
> Sholde be constant in adversitee
> As was Grisilde; therfore Petrak writeth
> This storie, which with heigh stile he enditeth.
>
> (1142–8)

During the course of his version, Chaucer intensifies this aspect of
the story by increasing the religious references and images in his
verse. The ideal goodness of Griselda is associated, to some extent,
with her upbringing, where poverty and hardship created in her
great moral strength (of the kind which we see in the poor widow in
'The Nun's Priest's Tale', and which is implied in the character of
the widow in 'The Prioress's Tale'). But Griselda's character is not
attributed solely to her social environment. It is also closely linked
with God. She represents the highest Christian virtues, and we are
told that God's grace has given these to her in her poverty, just as
he gives her new grace when he transforms her at the marriage:

> And shortly forth this tale for to chace,
> I seye that to this newe markysesse
> God hath swich favour sent hire of his grace,
> That it ne semed nat by liklynesse
> That she was born and fed in rudenesse,
> As in a cote or in an oxe-stalle,
> But norissed in an emperoures halle.
>
> (393–9)

Her virtues stand out all the more because much of the first part
of the poem is concerned with the secular values of politics and
authority. Walter has the qualities of a good ruler, but in other
respects he has faults:

> Therwith he was, to speke as of lynage,
> The gentilleste yborn of Lumbardye,
> A fair persone, and strong, and yong of age,
> And ful of honour and of curteisye;
> Discreet ynogh his contree for to gye,
> Save in somme thynges that he was to blame . . .
>   (71–6)

The association of Griselda with God and Christian values is
sustained by the frequent use of scriptural references. There is,
for example, an important comparison of Griselda with Job:

> Men speke of Job, and moost for his humblesse,
> As clerkes, whan hem list, konne wel endite . . .
>   (932–3)

The verse is full of such echoes, and this gives to it an emblematic
quality. This, indeed, is the main feature of the style, and it is
well illustrated in the description of the meeting of Griselda and
Walter at the doorway of the poor cottage:

> And as she wolde over hir thresshfold gon,
> The markys cam, and gan hire for to calle;
> And she set doun hir water pot anon,
> Biside the thresshfold, in an oxes stalle,
> And doun upon hir knes she gan to falle,
> And with sad contenance kneleth stille,
> Til she had herd what was the lordes wille.
>   (288–94)

Every phrase and idea in this short section is emblematic: we
are reminded of all that the cottage stands for, the poverty and
hardship, and the moral strength; and we are also invited to
think of the threshold of the cottage as the gateway to a new life.
More important, there are clear Scriptural echoes in the picture
of the water pot and the ox-stall which associate Griselda with
the Virgin Mary. The effect which this style achieves is similar to
that in 'The Prioress's Tale'. Realism is of secondary importance
to idealism, and consequently there is little of the closely woven

detail of Chaucer's later style in these two tales.[12] The style of
'The Clerk's Tale' is well-suited to the presentation of an ideal.
It is not dramatic, and Chaucer makes no attempt to surprise his
audience with the unexpected. On the contrary, the narrative
moves slowly through a series of carefully planned stages. There
is, however, some variety within the style, for it alternates between
simple dialogue and description on the one hand, and on the other
a more complicated assessment of religious ideas.

Chaucer's main concern is to produce a formal pattern in his
verse, and this he achieves by frequent use of certain important
words and phrases, and by the repetition of key ideas. The modern reader experiences some difficulty in appreciating this style,
which can seem almost naïve. But it is important to recognize
that Chaucer's choice is a deliberate one, for he has chosen the
pattern and style which is most appropriate to a Tale which does
not aim at realism at all, but rather at the celebration of an ideal.
Yet the Tale does, to some extent, contain realism. At various
stages in the Tale, Chaucer's interest in human life and behaviour
breaks through. There is little in Petrarch's original which
describes the motives and feelings of Griselda and Walter, but
Chaucer is not content to restrict himself in this way. He
attempts to make both Griselda and Walter real human beings as
well as religious symbols. One of the most striking examples of
this is Chaucer's intensification of the pathos of Griselda's
situation:

> But atte laste to speken she bigan,
> And mekely she to the sergeant preyde,
> So as he was a worthy gentil man,
> That she moste kisse hire child er that it deyde.
> And in hir barm this litel child she leyde
> With ful sad face, and gan the child to blisse,
> And lulled it, and after gan it kisse.
>
> (547–53)

We find the same kind of thing in the account of Griselda's
emotional response to the restoration of her children and her
reconciliation with her husband. A rather different example is
Chaucer's attempt to rationalize his Tale:

> He hadde assayed hire ynogh bifore,
> And foond hire evere good; what neded it

Hire for to tempte, and alwey moore and moore,
Though som men preise it for a subtil wit?
But as for me, I seye that yvele it sit
To assaye a wyf whan that it is no nede,
And putten hire in angwyssh and in drede.

(456–62)

This passage is not found in Petrarch's version, and it illustrates very well the problem which Chaucer creates for himself in this Tale. His appeal to reason concerns a story which is essentially irrational, both in its original folk-tale form and in Petrarch's symbolic version.

It can be seen that Chaucer's development of the human side of the story conflicts with the emblematic design of the whole.[13] He has made both Griselda and Walter too human, with the result that we pity, rather than praise, Griselda's patience, and condemn, for its psychological excess, Walter's cruelty. This reaction is something which cannot be changed by the knowledge that God's grace sustains Griselda in her suffering, and that Walter experiences secret repentance for his actions. What is more, this interest in the human aspect of the Tale which Chaucer cultivates leads us to a sense of dissatisfaction with his chosen verse style, which is entirely appropriate to the Tale as religious symbol but inadequate as a vehicle for the exploration of real human experience.

Chaucer clearly recognized the many difficulties which faced him in writing his version of Petrarch's poem. He tried a number of ways to solve the problems, and the most successful of these attempts may be found in the Clerk's Epilogue or Envoy to his Tale. It is true that he gives a simple, open statement of the moral purpose of the Tale: 'Lat us thanne lyve in vertuous suffraunce'. (1162). But he has much more to say. The style changes from the stylized to the colloquial and the Clerk turns back to reality after his long Tale about idealism:

But o word, lordynges, herkneth er I go:
It were ful hard to fynde now-a-dayes
In al a toun Grisildis thre or two;
For if that they were put to swiche assayes,
The gold of hem hath now so badde alayes
With bras, that thogh the coyne be fair at ye,
It wolde rather breste a-two than plye.

(1163–9)

He testifies that the truth of human experience is very different from the fairy-tale unreality of Griselda's extreme goodness. Yet this paradox does not invalidate all that Griselda represents, and the ironical tone which the Clerk adopts in the last six stanzas serves to emphasize still more her great worth. By pretending to dismiss the story he has told as idealistic nonsense, the Clerk establishes more clearly the superiority of Griselda over the violent conflicts and struggles which characterize those who demand ascendancy in marriage. The energetic rhythms and grotesque images give dramatic force to the strife of such relationships:

> O noble wyves, ful of heigh prudence,
> Lat noon humylitee youre tonge naille . . .
> Ye archewyves, stondeth at defense,
> Syn ye be strong as is a greet camaille;
> Ne suffreth nat that men yow doon offense.
> And sklendre wyves, fieble as in bataille,
> Beth egre as is a tygre yond in Ynde;
> Ay clappeth as a mille, I yow consaille . . .
> Be ay of chiere as light as leef on lynde,
> And lat hym care, and wepe, and wrynge, and waille!
>   (1183–4; 1195–1200; 1211–12)

This is a powerful challenge to that great champion of feminine emancipation, the Wife of Bath, and its biting irony leaves us in no doubt as to where the Clerk really stands.

Although it is complicated in structure and a little uneven in texture, 'The Clerk's Tale' is an impressive achievement. In it Chaucer tries to broaden the relevance of an old story, and he concerns himself with some interesting contemporary problems. In the final analysis, however, it is the vision of Griselda's perfection which remains uppermost in our minds. And it is this quality which links the Tale so closely with that of the Prioress, for although the complexity of the Clerk's narrative distinguishes it from the simple Saint's Legend, both Tales share a common purpose: the celebration, in symbolic form, of an ideal.

The Canon's Yeoman's Tale

This is the day, I am to perfect for him
The *magisterium*, our great work, the stone;
And yield it, made, into his hands: of which,
He has, this month, talk'd, as he were possess'd.
And now, he's dealing pieces on't away . . .
If his dream last, he'll turn the age to gold.
    (Ben Jonson: *The Alchemist*; Act I, scene 4)

Following the conclusion of the Second Nun's Tale of St Cecile, Chaucer surprises and puzzles his audience with a totally unexpected development. At Boughtoun under Blee the pilgrims are overtaken by two mysterious strangers who are riding along the Canterbury road in great haste. One of them is a cleric, a canon clothed wholly in black, and it is on him that Chaucer focuses attention. He is drenched with sweat, and his horse is heated and foam-flecked. He presents a strange figure, and the questioning stares of the pilgrims force him to offer some explanation for his hasty arrival:

> 'God save,' quod he, 'this joly compaignye!
> Faste have I priked,' quod he, 'for youre sake,
> By cause that I wolde yow atake,
> To riden in this myrie compaignye.'
>
> (583–6)

His companion, who seems to be a servant of some kind, is quick to add supporting details:

> His yeman eek was ful of curteisye,
> And seyde, 'Sires, now in the morwe-tyde
> Out of youre hostelrie I saugh yow ryde,
> And warned heer my lord and my soverayn,
> Which that to ryden with yow is ful fayn
> For his desport; he loveth daliaunce.'
>
> (587–92)

But there is something unconvincing about these comments. The pilgrims' journey which we have been following for some time has been conducted at a leisurely pace, and there seems little reason to believe that these two riders have been forced to spur at such speed simply in order to catch up with the band. After all, only five miles have been covered since the pilgrims set out from their overnight resting-place at Ospringe. What is more, it seems unlikely that this sombre and slovenly figure is at all interested in 'desport' and 'daliaunce' as the Yeoman states. His appearance and his awkward silence suggest the opposite. He lurks in the background while the Yeoman answers Harry

Bailly's searching questions. He clearly has something to hide, and as the Yeoman warms to his story he fears that his secret will be discovered. Unable to contain his guilty suspicions, he attempts to silence the man with a sinister criminal threat, but Harry Bailly has other plans, and to the Canon's dismay he encourages the Yeoman to reveal all. Fearing a complete betrayal, the Canon departs as hastily as he arrived, and rides out of the Tale.

The arrival of these two strangers poses a number of questions for us and the pilgrims. The most immediate is the problem of their identity, for although Chaucer pays close attention to the details of the black rider's clothing and his horse (as, indeed, he does in many of his descriptions in 'The General Prologue'), he only reveals his true identity gradually through a series of subtle hints. When we eventually realize that the Canon is, in fact, an alchemist, all the clues fit into place, and the sequence becomes clear. There are, for example, two important motifs which stand out at the opening of the Canon's Yeoman's Prologue. Chaucer emphasizes most of all the hot sweat on the riders and their horses, and it is this feature, reinforced with an apt simile taken from alchemy, which ends the description. All this suggests a hot, hasty ride under the warm spring sun, but it also recalls the heat of the alchemist's furnace and the sweaty atmosphere of the laboratory. The other motif is the idea of headlong speed. Chaucer conveys this through the excited rhythm of the verse and the repetition of the word 'priked', and the effect is intensified by the alliteration and the short, sharp syllables in these lines:

> Aboute the peytrel stood the foom ful hye;
> He was of foom al flekked as a pye.
>
> (564–5)

Although we are told that the black rider is a Canon, it is significant that this conclusion has only been reached after some deliberation:

> For which, whan I hadde longe avysed me,
> I demed hym som chanoun for to be.
>
> (572–3)

Much of the evidence, in fact, suggests something quite different, for his clothes are filthy and torn, he rides in irreverent haste,

and even the Summoner and the Pardoner, the lowest of the clerical characters, conduct themselves with more composure than this sweating figure. His dirty and undignified appearance arouses Harry Bailly's interest:

'His overslope nys nat worth a myte,
As in effect, to hym, so moot I go!
It is al baudy and totore also.
Why is thy lord so sluttissh, I the preye,
And is of power bettre clooth to beye,
If that his dede accorde with thy speche?'
(633–8)

The Canon's tattered clothing is not simply the result of his hard ride, and Harry Bailly is quick to draw perceptive conclusions about him. As with the descriptions in 'The General Prologue', the Canon's clothing gives important information about his character and status. He lacks self-respect and social charm (Harry Bailly's comments about wisdom and merriment, lines 595 and 596, are clearly ironic); and, most important, he lacks money, for the study of alchemy was an expensive pursuit: costly chemical ingredients and specialized apparatus were needed for experiments, and even the fuel to heat the furnaces was far from cheap. Chaucer's portrait is the traditional picture of the alchemist of the late fourteenth century, a man who came to be despised for his folly and hated for the criminal acts which his poverty often forced him to commit.

The hurried and sinister behaviour of the Canon suggests that, like the character in the Yeoman's Tale, he is a fugitive from justice. He probably owes large sums of money borrowed to finance his experiments. In addition, it seems likely that his hasty ride down the Canterbury road follows the successful completion of some fraudulent trickery. He travels light, and has no luggage which might encumber him, for his bag is folded double and is presumably empty:

A male tweyfoold on his croper lay;
It semed that he caried lite array.
(566–7)

He seems to be making good his escape before his victim dis-covers the truth. Chaucer provides other hints which support this idea: during the course of his conversation with Harry

Bailly, the Yeoman takes pains, in a suspicious parenthesis, to dissociate himself from his master's activities:

> 'But al his craft ye may nat wite at me,
> And somwhat helpe I yet to his wirkyng—'
>
> (621–2)

There is, too, the description of the dark, secret places where the Canon lives, and this associates him explicitly with thievery and deception:

> 'In the suburbes of a toun,' quod he,
> 'Lurkynge in hernes and in lanes blynde,
> Whereas thise robbours and thise theves by kynde
> Holden hir pryvee fereful residence,
> As they that dar nat shewen hir presence;
> So faren we, if I shal seye the sothe.'
>
> (657–62)

It is not surprising that the shrewd and realistic Harry Bailly has considerable misgivings about the activities and identities of the two strangers. He is far from satisfied by their initial explanations, and he conducts a searching interrogation of the Yeoman while at the same time skilfully encouraging him to talk openly for the entertainment of the company.

The mystery which surrounds the black rider is intensified by a number of darker associations of which Chaucer and his audience are plainly aware. The very colour of his clothing has sinister implications. It may be that he wears the black habit because he is a Black Canon, that is, a Canon Regular of St Augustine.[1] But black is also the colour of evil, and there was, in medieval times, a direct link between alchemy and the devil. The alchemist was engaged in the search for the Philosopher's Stone which would transmute quicksilver and copper into silver and gold. There was, however, a theoretical, spiritual aspect of alchemy, for the alchemist was also searching for the Great Elixir of Life which would bring eternal power and immortality. The spiritual alchemist was aspiring to the position of God, the creator of the world, for he was himself searching for the power of creation. Thus the alchemist offered a diabolic challenge to God, and this challenge is an aspect of the primary sin of pride by which Lucifer, aspiring to God's supremacy, fell to damnation. Because of this association with the devil, the alchemist was

considered to be in danger of losing his soul. Chaucer means us
to see his Canon as a lost soul, for his life is spent in futile wan-
derings and furtive secrecy, and he is condemned to gain no
reward for his activities save what he can obtain by fraud. In
view of this, it is peculiarly significant that Chaucer's alchemist
should be a cleric, and the irony would not have been lost on his
contemporary readers. Many clerics indulged in the practice of
this futile science in Chaucer's day, and his satirical portrait
implies an attack on all clerical alchemists who diverted their
energies from their true religious duties. Indeed, the pursuit
of alchemy by clerics may be seen as yet one more example of
the corruption of the Church in the late Middle Ages, and as
such Chaucer condemns it with the same subtle vigour as he
does the activities of the Pardoner and the Summoner.

Chaucer's satire is not, however, directed solely against clerical
alchemists. He is also concerned for the wider social problems
created and aggravated by the science. Alchemical research
wasted fuel and other valuable materials, and we know that it
frequently led to crime and increased existing social hardship and
poverty. Such evils were intolerable to thinking men, and an
attempt was made to stamp out the science in 1403 when it was
made illegal in England. It may be, therefore, that Chaucer
intended his portrait and tale to be part of a campaign for the
abolition of this particular social evil. And, indeed, he may well
have had an additional personal reason for attacking the problem,
for it has been suggested that he himself had been cheated by
an alchemist named William Shuchirch who was a canon of
King's Chapel, Windsor, and who is known to have practised
the science during Chaucer's lifetime.[2] Whether this specula-
tion has any foundation may be debated, but there can be no
question about Chaucer's attitude towards alchemy and those
who pursued it.

Much of what we learn about the Canon is revealed by the
Yeoman, and he himself is something of an enigma. His relationship with his master is puzzling. At first, in reply to Harry
Bailly's questions, he enthusiastically praises his master, and
recommends his wisdom and skill to the pilgrims:

'. . . also, sire, trusteth me,
And ye hym knewe as wel as do I,

Ye wolde wondre how wel and craftily
He koude werke, and that in sondry wise.'
(601–4)

The words seem genuine, and they are animated by a spon-
taneous, energetic rhythm. But there is the possibility of a
second meaning in the word 'craftily', and indeed it is not long
before the Yeoman is using this same word in a wholly pejorative
sense. The rhythm does not change when he replies to Harry
Bailly's question about his discoloured face, but the tone is quite
different from that of his earlier comments. The Yeoman is
critical of the futile work in which he assists, and the failure of
the alchemical research he plainly associates with his master:

'We blondren evere and pouren in the fir,
And for al that we faille of oure desir,
For evere we lakken oure conclusioun. . . .
But that science is so fer us biforn,
We mowen nat, although we hadden it sworn,
It overtake, it slit awey so faste.'
(670–2, 680–2)

He has been reduced to poverty and ill-health, and pent up
inside him lurks a violent hatred which soon erupts in a vigorous
tirade. It is as though the hasty departure of the Canon with-
draws the last restraint; the Yeoman cannot control his feelings,
and he gives them full rein as he curses his master:

'Syn he is goon, the foule feend hym quelle! . . .
He that me broghte first unto that game,
Er that he dye, sorwe have he and shame!'
(705, 708–9)

The Yeoman is not an expert in the science of alchemy, and
he knows only a fraction of his master's lore. But this does not
diminish the magnetic attraction of the search for the Great
Elixir. It is like a drug, and those addicted to it cannot turn aside
while there seems to be a remote chance of success. Simple
though he is, the servant knows he is caught in a trap:

'And yet, for al my smert and al my grief,
For al my sorwe, labour, and meschief,
I koude nevere leve it in no wise.'
(712–14)

As we have already seen, alchemy and the crime and poverty consequent on it were commonplace in the late fourteenth century. The Yeoman acknowledges that there are many who suffer as he does, but this offers little consolation. All he can do is warn others against alchemists, and this course he pursues with bitter irony as he feigns joyful enthusiasm in a rhetorical cry: 'Lo! which vantage is to multiplie!' (731). The rhythm of his words becomes slower, and with solemn yet simple emphasis he pronounces his conclusion:

> For so helpe me God, therby shal he nat wynne,
> But empte his purs, and make his wittes thynne.
>
> (740–1)

The extra syllables and short words of the first line give the dramatic impression that the sentiments catch in his throat, and he appears to be genuinely concerned at the fate of others who are similarly ensnared as he has been. Yet he himself seems reluctant to abandon the science, and as soon as he begins to recount some of the details of alchemical experiments the verse becomes lively and fast-moving again. He is fascinated by all that he has seen.

During the course of his time as servant to the Canon, the Yeoman has become acquainted with much of the terminology of alchemy.[3] He is obviously proud of this knowledge and he expends much time and energy in displaying it to the listening pilgrims. Like the Pardoner, he is carried away by the sound of his own voice. As he expounds his knowledge, the verse moves along at a great pace, animated with a vigorous rhythm, and the Yeoman skilfully employs the rhetorical device of multiplication of instances. Yet he would be a poor teacher, for he understands little of the significance of the information which he has learned by rote, and the effect of the long lists of details is quite bewildering. As the names pour from his lips, he creates a sense of confusion and lack of purpose which is entirely appropriate since the science itself is empty and valueless. But although he is ignorant, he is no fool, and he recognizes full well that his understanding of the subject is very limited:

> Though I by ordre hem nat reherce kan,
> By cause that I am a lewed man,
> Yet wol I telle hem as they come to mynde,

> Thogh I ne kan nat sette hem in hir kynde . . .
> (786–9)

He is also well aware that the pursuit of alchemy is futile and degrading. All that is done is useless, as Chaucer's repeated negatives show:

> For alle oure sleightes we kan nat conclude.
> Oure orpyment and sublymed mercurie . . .
> Noght helpeth us, oure labour is in veyn.
> Ne eek oure spirites ascencioun,
> Ne oure materes that lyen al fix adoun,
> Mowe in oure werkyng no thyng us availle,
> For lost is al oure labour and travaille . . .
> (773–4, 777–81)

The Yeoman's account of the everyday things which are employed in alchemical research produces an effect of revulsion, and we are compelled to recall the dirty and undignified figure of the Canon with which the episode began:

> Unslekked lym, chalk, and gleyre of an ey,
> Poudres diverse, asshes, donge, pisse, and cley,
> Cered pokkets, sal peter, vitriole,
> And diverse fires maad of wode and cole;
> Sal tartre, alkaly, and sal preparat,
> And combust materes and coagulat;
> Cley maad with hors or mannes heer, and oille
> Of tartre, alum glas, berme, wort, and argoille . . .
> (806–13)

The passage emphasizes the folly of the whole science, and it seems that the Yeoman is aware of this, to some extent, for his voice falters, and the rhythm of the verse becomes broken and confused. But his dramatic display of self-pity (in which he indulges at intervals during the Prologue) is soon over. He has much more to tell, and the vigour returns as he moves on to a very different aspect of alchemy. Although he is anxious to entertain his listeners again, he has even less idea of the implications of this new information. For although he is talking about the important metals and chemicals on which alchemy is based, we are reminded of the connection between the practical science and astrology. From here it is but a short step to the more abstract and sinister implications of alchemy, namely the search for the

Great Elixir of Life, and the diabolic challenge to God's omnipotence, which we discussed earlier. Other hints of this follow
in the ironic use of the image of the Bible: 'To tellen al wolde
passen any bible / That owher is' (857–8), and, more explicitly,
in the idea of the raising up of devils:

> For, as I trowe, I have yow toold ynowe
> To reyse a feend, al looke he never so rowe.
> (860–1)

Also, a little later, we are conscious of a double force in the smell
of brimstone, traditionally symbolic of hell-fires. That the Yeoman has no understanding of this aspect of his master's study is
made clear by his continued preoccupation, not with spiritual
danger, but with material poverty:

> This cursed craft whoso wole excercise,
> He shal no good han that hym may suffise;
> For al the good he spendeth theraboute
> He lese shal; therof have I no doute.
> (830–3)

The result, he assures us, is the same for the wise and the foolish.
This over-simplified conclusion is an artless repetition by the
Yeoman of his attitude. He is basically ignorant, and his mind
is limited and disorganized. Chaucer skilfully reveals this through
the constant repetitions and false starts throughout the Prologue. Often the Yeoman seems to be on the point of ending his
confession, and turning to his Tale, when some new aspect of
alchemy comes to mind and forces him to begin again: 'Yet forgat I to maken rehersaille / Of watres corosif' (852–3). This
gives added realism to the portrait, and it seems that we are
watching a real person.

Time and again Chaucer offers a glimpse of the workings of
the Yeoman's mind. One of the most prominent examples of
this psychological investigation comes with the Yeoman's statement of the addictive nature of alchemy. It brings poverty and
sorrow, but the alchemist continues to grasp at his tenuous
hopes, abandoning companions and happiness in the process.
The influence of alchemy is paradoxical: 'For unto hem it is a
bitter sweete' (878)—but the paradox is clear enough for the
Yeoman to recognize. All who come into contact with alchemy
are tainted by it. The alchemist pursues his study with a relish

akin to sexual lust, a parallel which Chaucer deliberately suggests in the use of 'goot', 'rammissh' and 'hoot', traditional lustful terms. And the secretive, treacherous attitude of the alchemist reminds us of the Canon who fled away for fear of discovery.

At this stage in the Prologue the Yeoman appears to be about to turn to his Tale, but instead his mind wanders again and he begins to give an account of the conduct of an experiment in his master's laboratory. His description is presented with great vigour, and there is a fascinating vitality in the picture of the pots leaping violently into the air, as if endowed with a magical life of their own:

> Thise metals been of so greet violence,
> Oure walles mowe nat make hem resistence,
> But if they weren wroght of lym and stoon;
> They percen so, and thurgh the wal they goon.
> And somme of hem synken into the ground—
> Thus han we lost by tymes many a pound—
> And somme are scatered al the floor aboute;
> Somme lepe into the roof.
>
> (908–15)

There is, in this passage, the same kind of sinister energy that we have already associated with the Canon's hasty arrival and departure, and with the enthusiastic but disorderly vigour of the Yeoman's confession. At the same time, the apparent life within the pots and the metals themselves reminds us of the medieval belief that all things inclined upwards towards a more perfect state. This idea is based on the familiar concept of Order within the universe; all things were inter-related in the great Scale of Being, and were therefore part of the grand design of 'God, Architect, Artist, and Monarch', who 'himself guarantees the goodness, truth and beauty of the being and order of the world.'[4] Consequently all things looked towards ultimate perfection. Minerals, like all matter, belonged to a chain of order. Gold was the perfection of this chain, and all other metals were merely stages in the production of gold. The hope of the alchemist was based on the belief that man could assist and quicken a process in which quicksilver and copper, for example, were already engaged. The hope was, of course, false; but it is not difficult to imagine how such an idea came to exercise such an influence in the Middle Ages, and to this the Yeoman testifies most dramatically.

Much of his confession takes the form of a simple description of the materials and processes of alchemical research. Chaucer concludes the Prologue, however, with a different technique, that of reported dialogue. Here the drama of the situation is heightened by the inclusion of snatches of conversation. The Yeoman must often have witnessed a quarrel between his master and his associates, and he captures all the folly and mutual recrimination which ensue from such a disastrous end to the experiments. There is a lively rhythm in the dialogue, and particularly apt is the analogy with another aspect of medieval life, the hazards of the merchant whose prosperity depended on the seas and winds (We recall the same kind of reference in one of the *exempla* of 'The Nun's Priest's Tale'[5]). Perhaps less real and immediate is the concluding verse paragraph. The Yeoman is at pains again to emphasize the empty futility of the science: 'We faille of that which that we wolden have', but his former vigour is weakened by his recourse at this late stage to proverbial clichés. He seems to have exhausted his confession (something which never happens to the Pardoner), and so quickly turns to his Tale.

In structure the Tale is quite straightforward. The story itself is divided into three parts, the three tricks which the Canon employs to beguile his victim, the gullible priest. This narrative is set within two moralizing sections, and it is clear that the three anecdotes are intended as *exempla*, or illustrations of the basic theme. Once again, Chaucer is making use of the medieval rhetorical conventions, and the Yeoman's method is similar to that of the Pardoner. The Tale may also be seen as an example of the medieval *fabliau* tradition, with its rhythmic energy, coarse humour and foolish victim.

The Tale opens with an introduction to the chief character, who bears a remarkable resemblance to the Yeoman's former master. The Yeoman's purpose is not, however, to describe this Canon's personal appearance, but rather to give some indication of his moral attributes. Evil and deceit are the predominant impressions, and this is supported by the reference to the great cities which fell to destruction, and by the analogy of the Canon to a treacherous serpent and to the devil:

> For in his termes he wol hym so wynde,
> And speke his wordes in so sly a kynde,

Whanne he commune shal with any wight,
That he wol make hym doten anonright,
But it a feend be, as hymselven is.

(980–4)

We now expect that the Yeoman will proceed directly to his Tale, but his confused mind leads him to a further digression. There are, as we know, among the company of the pilgrims a number of clerics. Lest they should take offence at the principal character of his Tale the Yeoman tries to dissociate any of his audience from the corrupt Canon, although, ironically, much of what we have seen of many of the pilgrim clerics suggests that the Yeoman's protestations may well conceal an apt parallel.

The Yeoman's explanation of the moral purpose of his Tale displays Chaucer's cutting irony. It is the biblical *exempla* which give to the Yeoman's comments this double edge, for we are asked to recall Judas, the traitor. The Yeoman intends his audience to associate this with the treachery of the Canon to his religious order and also to the priest whom he fools. But the Yeoman forgets that he himself is a traitor, since he has betrayed the secrets of his master. Like the Pardoner, he is condemned out of his own mouth.

When the first character of the Tale has been introduced, the Yeoman turns to the priest. It is essential to the story that the priest should be greedy and covetous, and this is how he is presented. The brief portrait is made more emphatic by the inclusion of an element of satirical criticism, for the priest is not a good pastor, but an idle lover of pleasure, an 'annueleer', of whom Chaucer had a very low opinion as lte made clear in the section on the Parson in 'The General Prologue':

He sette nat his benefice to hyre
And leet his sheep encombred in the myre
And ran to Londoun unto Seinte Poules
To seken hym a chaunterie for soules,
Or with a bretherhed to been withholde;
But dwelte at hoom, and kepte wel his folde,
So that the wolf ne made it nat myscarie;
He was a shepherde and noght a mercenarie.

(507–14)

The initial meeting of the two characters is described in a simple and direct way. The verse moves fast, and it is but a short

time before we find ourselves plunged into the centre of the
Canon's trickery. The interest is now focussed on the characters
and their personalities, and so Chaucer changes from reported
narrative to direct, dramatic dialogue. The Canon's flattering
trickery is quite clever, but it is interesting that the words he
uses are simple. At one point, however, he employs a rhetorical
device, that of *exclamatio*:

> O sely preest! o sely innocent!
> With coveitise anon thou shalt be blent!
> O gracelees, ful blynd is thy conceite,
> No thyng ne artow war of the deceite
> Which that this fox yshapen hath to thee!
>
> (1076–80)

It is significant that this should be used when the narrative seems
to be reaching a climax, but the Yeoman lacks the skill of the
Pardoner or the Nun's Priest, and the effect is lost when he suddenly follows another train of thought and attempts to differentiate between his former master and the character in his Tale.
Much debate has centred on this problem, for it is difficult to
decide whether or not the Yeoman is to be believed. It does seem,
however, that much of the point of the Tale is lost if we do accept
the Yeoman's explanation. The violent hatred he displayed for
his master in the Prologue is not altogether absent from the
Tale. There are a number of short phrases which show how
irrepressible this hatred is: 'the foule feend hym fecche!', 'with
sory grace!' and 'yvele moot he cheeve!'; and at one point in
particular the Yeoman is carried away by his emotions and utters
a terrible curse:

> —the devel out of his skyn
> Hym terve, I pray to God, for his falshede!
> For he was evere fals in thoght and dede—
>
> (1273–5)

A valuable unity is added to the whole sequence if we assume
that both Prologue and Tale concern the same villain. It is
certainly likely that the Yeoman's master had indulged in the
kind of sharp practice recounted in the Tale, and there is a striking similarity between the black Canon and the character in the
Tale in these lines:

On his falshede fayn wolde I me wreke,
If I wiste how, but he is heere and there;
He is so variaunt, he abit nowhere.

(1173-5)

Although the Canon's tricks are elaborately planned and
executed, it is not difficult to follow the details in each case. And
we presume, in any case, that these tales are traditional stories
which would be familiar to many of Chaucer's contemporaries,
especially in view of the growing disrepute into which alchemy
was falling. Yet the rather unintelligent Yeoman takes great pains
to ensure that every action is made clear to the audience. He fails
to realize that the pilgrims can follow his Tale with great ease,
and they are likely to find more significance in what he says than
he himself has recognized.

The preparation for the alchemical experiments are under-
taken with foolish enthusiasm, and Chaucer conveys this sense
in the breathless speed of the description and the repetition of
the conjunction 'and'. The priest, whose wealth is being squan-
dered, plays an active role in this action, and it is appropriate
that he should. Not only does this add to the irony of the story,
but it also accords with the *fabliau* tradition, in which the victim
willingly and actively assisted in his own ruin. During the course
of the experiments, the Canon encourages the priest to take part.
When the worthless powder is thrown into the pot in the first
experiment, he invites the priest to help:

'For in tokenyng I thee love,'
Quod this chanoun, 'thyne owene handes two
Shul werche al thyng which that shal heer be do.'

(1153-5)

And in the final experiment, the priest himself draws out the
silver. The irony of the willing participation is particularly clear
when the Canon pursuades the priest to purchase, from his own
pocket, the materials required. Little sympathy for the foolish
priest is intended in this Tale, for he is a conventional comic
figure who must be the object of ridicule. At the conclusion of
the final experiment, Chaucer inserts a parenthesis which further
mocks the priest:

This sotted preest, who was gladder than he?
Was nevere brid gladder agayn the day,

Ne nyghtyngale, in the sesoun of May,
Was nevere noon that luste bet to synge;
Ne lady lustier in carolynge,
Or for to speke of love and wommanhede,
Ne knyght in armes to doon an hardy dede,
To stonden in grace of his lady deere,
Than hadde this preest this soory craft to leere.
(1341–9)

This is the language of Courtly Love, and as such it is totally
out of place. Yet Chaucer's purpose is clear enough, for he offers
an ironic comparison between delight in love on the one hand,
and on the other limitless greed and lust for power. The arti-
ficiality of this passage provides a useful structural break before
the quick, colloquial dialogue with which the Tale concludes. The
successful completion of the trickery follows with swift inevitability, just like the more terrifying conclusion of 'The Pardoner's
Tale'. And while the victim is still gloating over his apparent
good fortune, the Canon disappears, and is never seen again.

When the Yeoman has reached the end of his Tale, the pace of
the verse becomes slower, and the tone more thoughtful. The
moral of the story is insistently repeated, and its impact is
assisted by the use of three conventional rhetorical figures.
Exclamatio is used, though in a very simple way, as we would
expect from the unlearned servant:

Lo! swich a lucre is in this lusty game . . .
O! fy, for shame! they that han been brent,
Allas! kan they nat flee the fires heete?
(1402, 1407–8)

There is nothing unusual about this, and it is not the first time
that the Yeoman has displayed a little knowledge of this rhetorical
device. Secondly, he attempts to intensify the impact of his moral
by listing a number of proverbs, or *sententiae*. This technique
is more effective here than when the Yeoman tried it previously
at the conclusion of his Prologue. There is, for example, an
important organic link between the Tale itself and the image of
the fire in one of the proverbs: 'Withdraweth the fir, lest it to
faste brenne'. What is more difficult to accept is the third rhetorical device employed by the Yeoman, that of *exempla*. The
allusions and authoritative references to Arnold of the Newe

Toun, Hermes, Senior and Plato are more suited to Chaucer's mouth than to the Yeoman, and it seems that, at this point in the concluding sequence, Chaucer lays aside his mask and speaks directly to his audience. This would be particularly appropriate if, as has been suggested, Chaucer himself had been tricked by an alchemist, or if the Tale is Chaucer's contribution to the campaign against alchemy. And the choice of references is entirely apt, revealing Chaucer's interest in alchemy and its effect in late fourteenth-century society.

This change of focus which Chaucer uses at the conclusion of the Tale offers some searching questions to the more learned of his contemporaries. We are, in particular, reminded again of the darker side of alchemical research, and the possibility of damnation inherent within the search for the Great Elixir of Life. But against this diabolic quest is set the omnipotence of God, and a positive consolation is offered to the man who, though he may lose all earthly wealth, turns at last to God and achieves a heavenly reward. It may be that this conclusion is only a convention,[6] but it offers a fitting comment on the Yeoman's former master, and its telling irony would not have been lost on all the pilgrims.

The Franklin's Tale

Considryng eke how I hange in balaunce,
In your service, such, lo! is my chaunce,
Abidyng grace, whan that your gentilnesse,
Of my grete wo listeth don alleggeaunce,
And wyth your pite me som wise avaunce,
In ful rebatyng of myn hevynesse,
And thynketh by resoun that wommanly noblesse
Shulde nat desire for to do the outrance
Ther as she fyndeth non unbuxumnesse.

      (Chaucer: 'Womanly Noblesse': lines 18–26)

The portrait of the Franklin in 'The General Prologue' depicts a wealthy country squire, not of noble lineage himself but, nevertheless, a landowner in his own right holding his property free from feudal obligations. He was a sociable man whose table 'stood redy covered al the longe day' to welcome any unexpected guest, and

> To lyven in delit was evere his wone,
> For he was Epicurus owene sone . . .
>
> (335–6)

He combined this love of the good life with great administrative and professional ability: he was a presiding magistrate, had been a knight of the shire, and therefore a member of parliament, and an auditor of taxes, and now he was travelling to Canterbury in the company of the Sergeant of the Law, a distinguished and high-ranking barrister. However, in spite of his wealth and patronage the Franklin was still a commoner and was, therefore, understandably conscious of his social status: he admired the story-tellers from amongst the nobility such as the Knight and his son the Squire of whose 'speche I have greet deyntee' and expressed his disappointment that his own son

> '. . . hath levere talken with a page
> Than to comune with any gentil wight
> Where he myghte lerne gentillesse aright.'
>
> (692–4)

Such is the character of the teller of the Tale, and it is clear that Chaucer, who had himself been a knight of the shire, had considerable sympathy for the Franklin and admired his way of life. The Franklin's temperament ('Of his complexioun he was sangwyn') is wholly suited not only to the Tale which he is to tell but also to resolve the animosities which had arisen amongst the travellers, who were, after all, on a religious pilgrimage; and also to attempt to restore the tone of the Tales to the dignity of the opening one, for the Knight's elegant tale of courtly lovers was followed by the bawdy stories of the Miller, the Reeve and

the Cook. The Wife of Bath then advocated that in any harmonious marriage-relationship the wife should always be the dominant partner and mocked the whole teaching of the Church on marriage by justifying her own voluptuousness and by condemning celibacy. The Miller and the Reeve had told tales at the expense of each other and now the Wife in expressing her unorthodox views, albeit under a cloak of joviality, was also to take an unfair advantage of the ascetic Clerk by explaining in her prologue that her fifth husband had been a 'clerk of Oxenford' whom she had delighted to embarrass in front of her female friends, making

> . . . his face often reed and hoot
> For verray shame. . .

We can imagine the unworldly Clerk's feelings as he listened to the Wife of Bath indulging in her exhibitionism, and when his turn came to tell his Tale he reversed the situation and told a story of a dictatorial husband's domination over a subservient wife. 'The Merchant's Tale' about the infidelity of a child bride who takes advantage of her husband's blindness, castigates the whole institution of matrimony and so the Squire is called upon to redress the balance and restore the standard originally set by the Knight. He is asked to 'sey somwhat of love', but his narrative, summarized by Milton in 'Il Penseroso', becomes so involved that he proves himself totally incapable of fulfilling his task and his Tale is left unfinished.

And so to the Franklin. In his consideration of the *Canterbury Tales* as a connected Human Comedy rather than a series of isolated stories, Professor G. L. Kittredge[1] shows how the Franklin has the final word in what has been called the Marriage Debate, and although he may have exaggerated his case a little, nevertheless, the Franklin resolved the acrimony of the pilgrims and told a dignified story in a dignified manner. 'All art,' writes Northrop Frye, 'is equally conventionalized, but we do not ordinarily notice this fact unless we are unaccustomed to the convention,' and he continues to point out that the conventionalizing forces of modern literature often go unrecognized and make it 'difficult to appraise the literature of Chaucer, much of whose poetry is translated or paraphrased from others'.[2]

The convention of Courtly Love was the central theme of

'The Knight's Tale' and it also plays an important part in 'The Franklin's Tale'. Emanating from Ovid's *Ars Amatoria*, through to the Troubadour Poetry of the twelfth century, Courtly Love was given detailed literary consideration in the long French allegorical love poem the *Roman de la Rose* part of which Chaucer himself translated. Professor C. S. Lewis described Courtly Love as follows:

> The sentiment, of course, is love, but love of a highly specialised sort, whose characteristics may be enumerated as Humility, Courtesy, Adultery, and the Religion of Love. The Lover is always abject. Obedience to his lady's lightest wish, however whimsical, and silent acquiescence in her rebukes, however unjust, are the only virtues he dares to claim. There is a service of love closely modelled on the service which a feudal vassal owes to his lord. The lover is the lady's 'man'. He addresses her as midons, which etymologically represents not 'my lady' but 'my lord'. The whole attitude has been rightly described as a 'feudalization of love'. This solemn amatory ritual is felt to be part and parcel of the courtly life. It is possible only to those who are, in the old sense of the word, polite. It thus becomes, from one point of view the flower, from another the seed, of all those noble usages which distinguish the gentle from the vilein: only the courteous can love, but it is love that makes them courteous. Yet this love, though neither playful nor licentious in its expression, is always what the nineteenth century called 'dishonourable' love. The poet normally addresses another man's wife, and the situation is so carelessly accepted that he seldom concerns himself much with her husband: his real enemy is the rival. But if he is ethically careless, he is no lighthearted gallant: his love is represented as a despairing and tragical emotion—or almost despairing, for he is saved from complete wanhope by his faith in the God of Love who never betrays his faithful worshippers and who can subjugate the cruellest beauties.[3]

This Courtly Love convention flourished in a feudal society in which marriages were essentially those of convenience, when the wife was subjugated entirely to the domination of her husband and looked upon as part of his property; and in an age when the teaching of the Church was opposed to all forms of romantic love whether conducted within marriage or outside it.

'The Franklin's Tale' contains the inevitable triangle of husband, wife and lover, and using all the vocabulary of the Courtly Love Code the Franklin first describes the courting of Dorigen by Arveragus stressing 'his wo, his peyne, and his distresse'

which is the lover's traditional plight, but, of course, as the aim
of this courtship is marriage it is not strictly in accord with the
tradition. When after a year or so of married life Arveragus, the
husband, leaves his native Brittany for England 'To seke in
armes worshipe and honour', the courtly lover Aurelius is introduced and he is in the true *Roman de la Rose* tradition: it is the
month of May, Dorigen is in a garden and we are told that he:

> Hadde loved hire best of any creature
> Two yeere and moore, as was his aventure,
> But nevere dorste he tellen hire his grevaunce.
>
> (939–41)

Aurelius's behaviour closely parallels that of Arcite in 'The
Knight's Tale'.

It was in accord with convention for the poet to acknowledge
some earlier authority in order to give greater credence to his
arguments. Frequently Chaucer is content with a mere generalized 'As olde stories tellen us', but here he goes out of his way
to relate this tale to a specific literary genre:

> Thise olde gentil Britouns in hir dayes
> Of diverse aventures maden layes,
> Rymeyed in hir first Briton tonge;
> Whiche layes with hir instrumentz they songe,
> Or elles redden hem for hir plesaunce,
> And oon of hem have I in remembraunce . . .
>
> (709–14)

The precise literary source of 'The Franklin's Tale' is uncertain;
there are similarities to be found in Boccaccio, but there is no
reliable evidence that it comes from a Breton Lay such as were
collated by Marie de France at the end of the twelfth century.
There are, however, certain affinities with this genre: Courtly
Love, magic, and 'gentil' characters introduced as impersonal
types rather than as individuals. For example, Aurelius is first
mentioned as 'a squier' and only some twelve lines later do we
learn his name, while Dorigen is 'oon the faireste under sonne'.

In none of the other tales is the geographical setting more
important. 'Thise grisly feendly rokkes blake' are an integral
part of 'The Franklin's Tale' and by locating his story so precisely in Brittany where such rocks are a characteristic of the
coastline, Chaucer endows his Tale with the necessary realism

right from the first line. The Tale itself begins with an appropriate archaic reference to Brittany as Armorik.

Early in his prologue the Franklin emphasizes how conscious he is of his social status and we are again aware of how well the tone of the Tale is suited to the character of the teller.

> But, sires, by cause I am a burel man,
> At my bigynnyng first I yow biseche,
> Have me excused of my rude speche.
> I lerned nevere rethorik, certeyn. . . .
>
> (716–19)

This excuse that he is not well versed in rhetoric, which was one of the 'seven liberal arts' of the medieval scholastic curriculum covered by any educated gentleman, is, of course, no more substantiated than is Othello's 'Rude am I in speech', when so often that speech soars to unparalleled heights of nobility and eloquence; and, in the same way, 'The Franklin's Tale' contains examples of all the recognized 'colours' and 'tropes' of rhetoric. Indeed, his very apology is itself an example of *diminutio* the recognized device for engaging the reader's sympathy from the outset and is a part of the teaching of Geoffroi de Vinsauf (the 'Gaufred, deere maister soverayn' of 'The Nun's Priest's Tale'), whose *Nova Poetria* in the early part of the thirteenth century was used as a manual for poets writing in an elevated style. Charles Muscatine says: 'Chaucer in the *Canterbury Tales* seems very conscious of rhetoric. It is one of the subjects (like women and marriage) that he is forever making jokes about.'[4] And A. C. Spearing in commenting on the description of nightfall after Aurelius has been set his apparently hopeless task:

> But sodeynly bigonne revel newe
> Til that the brighte sonne loste his hewe;
> For th'orisonte hath reft the sonne his lyght,—
> This is as muche to seye as it was nyght!—
>
> (1015–18)

says that 'from one point of view this is a burel man's humorously deflating comment on the pretensions of rhetoric'.[5] Chaucer had satirized the *Nova Poetria* in 'The Nun's Priest's Tale' and the excessive use of rhetoric in 'The Franklin's Tale' and also in 'The Merchant's Tale' gives some weight to the belief that the very long

list in Dorigen's Complaint of the women who have preferred
death rather than dishonour is another instance of Chaucer's mild
scoffing at the 'art'. Much critical ink has, indeed, been expended
in condemning the unsatisfactory style of Dorigen's Complaint,
notably that it lacks an integrated form, and the lines:

> Now sith that maydens hadden swich despit
> To been defouled with mannes foul delit,
> Wel oghte a wyf rather hirselven slee
> Than be defouled, as it thynketh me.
>
> (1395–8)

do appear to indicate the closing of the list of *exempla*. But, as
James Sledd points out in his interesting essay,[6] this passage is
in fact not a conclusion but a transition from a discussion of
virtuous maids to virtuous wives, for Dorigen then goes on to
cite the stories of Hasdrubal's wife and Lucrece. There is then
a return to maids in the sixth *exemplum* which is immediately
followed by:

> Mo than a thousand stories, as I gesse,
> Koude I now telle as touchynge this mateere . . .
>
> (1412–14)

which one would expect to be Dorigen's last word on the subject.
But, not at all, she then continues for another forty-three lines
of further examples of virtuous maids and wives who contem-
plated suicide rather than be dishonoured, and shortly after her
resumption of the list gives yet another hint that she is about to
finish with:

> I wol conclude that it is bet for me
> To sleen myself than been defouled thus.
>
> (1422–3)

James Sledd notices a striking parallel in the rhetorical 'Nun's
Priest's Tale' when Chauntecleer begins his speech to Pertelote
on the significance of dreams and gives two lengthy examples to
illustrate his view followed by the apparent conclusion of:

> And therfore, faire Pertelote so deere,
> By swiche ensamples olde maistow leere'
> That no man sholde been to recchelees
> Of dremes; for I seye thee, doutelees,
> That many a dreem ful soore is for to drede.
>
> (*NPT* 3105–9)

In fact Chauntecleer goes on to give a further list of examples interspersed with similar apparently concluding lines as Dorigen makes in her Complaint.

We can accept more readily the skilfully ordered rhetoric of the impassioned pleas by Dorigen to 'Eterne God' and the later one to Fortune where the 'colours' and 'tropes' follow one another in such rich profusion and where, as also in parts of 'The Knight's Tale', we are more convinced of the poet's sincerity than we are in the more artificial (or so it seems to us, at any rate) hotchpotch of *exempla* in the Complaint; but due allowance must be made not only for the medieval reader's fondness for a conventionally bulky manuscript but also, since the oral tradition of poetry was still very strong, for the great delight of the medieval listener in a series of names pleasing to the ear. Further, as with the digressions in 'The Nun's Priest's Tale', Dorigen's Complaint is dramatically a perfectly legitimate method of holding up the action immediately before the denouément. To understand Dorigen's Complaint it must be viewed against this background of convention, and consideration taken of its place in the whole structure of 'The Franklin's Tale' and its relationship to the theme of *gentillesse*.[7]

Arveragus woos Dorigen and she agrees 'To take hym for hir housbonde and hir lord' while for his part:

> Of his free wyl he swoor hire as a knyght
> That nevere in al his lyf he, day ne nyght,
> Ne sholde upon hym take no maistrie
> Agayn hir wyl, ne kithe hire jalousie,
> But hire obeye, and folwe hir wyl in al,
> As any lovere to his lady shal,
> Save that the name of soveraynetee,
> That wolde he have for shame of his degree.
>
> (745-52)

And

> She seyde, 'Sire, sith of youre gentillesse
> Ye profre me to have so large a reyne,
> Ne wolde nevere God bitwixe us tweyne,
> As in my gilt, were outher werre or stryf.'
>
> (754-7)

The ideal marriage relationship is suggested here in which the parties attempt to obtain the best of both worlds by continuing to indulge in a Courtly Love partnership with Arveragus promising to 'hire obeye, and folwe hir wyl in al', and, at the same time, to have a conventional marriage arrangement with Dorigen as the 'humble trewe wyf'. And so this unorthodox position is made clear from the beginning, that love 'wol nat been constreyned by maistrye'. This is of particular importance here for two reasons: it emphasizes the theme of marriage in the Tale, and it also stresses the real love that Arveragus and Dorigen clearly had for each other, a love which transcends the barriers of convention and without which, of course, Arveragus's insistence at the end that Dorigen should keep her promise to Aurelius would have little dramatic force. In emphasizing this love Chaucer diverges noticeably from *Il Filocolo*, a suggested source of 'The Franklin's Tale' in which Dorigen's counterpart is presented by Boccaccio as showing very little wifely care or concern for her husband. It is not insignificant that Arveragus's concern for his social reputation here ('for shame of his degree') is also reiterated at the time of his insistence to Dorigen that she should keep her vow when he begs her 'To no wight telle thou of this aventure' (1483). It was noticed when considering Chaucer's portrait of the Franklin that he was himself very conscious of his own social status and this is emphasized throughout the Tale by the constant reference to *gentillesse*.

Gentillesse as a term is capable of many interpretations: in a limited way it embodies the idea of *noblesse oblige* and it will be remembered that it is what the class-conscious Franklin had hoped his own son might learn, and it is the quality the Franklin admired in 'The Squire's Tale' which prompted the Host's abrupt interjection, 'Straw for youre gentillesse'. It was 'namely the gentils everichon' who most appreciated 'The Knight's Tale', and it is the 'gentil Britouns' whom the Franklin addresses. The word can refer to ethical virtue and have a Christian spiritual connotation. 'The Franklin's Tale' embraces all these interpretations and a further shade of meaning is to be found in the Franklin's final question: 'Which was the mooste fre, as thynketh yow?' (1622). In the passage quoted above Dorigen refers to Arveragus's *gentillesse* in declining to assert his *maistrie* in the marriage. None of the characters fulfils this ideal of *gentillesse*

as completely as Arveragus whose insistence that Dorigen should keep her promise undoubtedly constitutes the extreme of all *gentillesse*. A. C. Spearing makes the interesting comment that 'at this crucial point *maistrie* re-enters the marriage, with an emphasis that gains force from the paradox by which Arveragus uses his *maistrie* to order his wife to keep her promise to become someone else's mistress'.[8]

After a year or more of married life in which Arveragus was to Dorigen both 'servant in love and lord in mariage' the husband leaves for a two-year visit to England 'To seke in armes worshipe and honour'. Dorigen 'that loveth hire housbonde as hire hertes lyf' was grief-stricken without him, and her friends' efforts to comfort her were in vain. She lived close to the shore and the sight of the sea and the passing ships, but more especially, 'thise grisly feendly rokkes blake' proved a constant reminder to her of her husband's absence and his peril, so that she was prompted to call upon:

'Eterne God, that thurgh thy purveiaunce
Ledest the world by certein governaunce,
In ydel, as men seyn, ye no thyng make.
But, Lord, thise grisly feendly rokkes blake,
That semen rather a foul confusion
Of werk than any fair creacion
Of swich a parfit wys God and a stable,
Why han ye wroght this werk unresonable?
For by this werk, south, north, ne west, ne eest,
Ther nys yfostred man, ne bryd, ne beest;
It dooth no good, to my wit, but anoyeth.
Se ye nat, Lord, how mankynde it destroyeth?
An hundred thousand bodyes of mankynde
Han rokkes slayn, al be they nat in mynde,
Whiche mankynde is so fair part of thy werk
That thou it madest lyk to thyn owene merk.
Thanne semed it ye hadde a greet chiertee
Toward mankynde; but how thanne may it bee
That ye swiche meenes make it to destroyen,
Whiche meenes do no good, but evere anoyen?
I woot wel clerkes wol seyn as hem leste,
By argumentz, that al is for the beste,
Though I ne kan the causes nat yknowe.
But thilke God that made wynd to blowe

As kepe my lord! this my conclusion.
To clerkes lete I al disputison.
But wolde God that alle thise rokkes blake
Were sonken into helle for his sake!
Thise rokkes sleen myn herte for the feere.'

(865–93)

In the light of subsequent events the metaphysical content of this
apostrophe to God is another of the paradoxes of the story; it is
very similar to Palamon's questioning of the Almighty in 'The
Knight's Tale'. The literary authority for this form of invocation
is to be found in the *De Consolatione Philosophiae* of Boethius,
which Chaucer had himself translated, in which Boethius in a
dialogue with his 'nurse Philosophy' (who states that what is, is
good) questions why God allows the lives of humans to be gov-
erned by Fortune. Chaucer translates:

> O thou governour, governynge alle thynges by certein ende, whi
> refusestow oonly to governe the werkes of men by duwe manere?
> Why suffrestow that slydynge Fortune turneth so grete enter-
> chaungynges of thynges; so that anoyous peyne, that scholde
> duweliche punysche felons, punysscheth innocentz? . . . Thow
> governour, withdraugh and restreyne the ravysschynge flodes, and
> fastne and ferme thise erthes stable with thilke boond by which thou
> governest the hevene that is so large.

Dorigen's personal concern is for control over these 'ravysschynge
flodes' and it is, of course, to Fortune that she makes her later
appeal for a solution to her problem. Although Chaucer is asking
the same philosophical question in each case, the prose version
of *Boece* bears little comparison stylistically with the much more
dramatically effective verse of Dorigen's apostrophe, containing
as it does some of the most profound and heartfelt lines in the
whole of the Tale.

Reference has already been made to the rhetoric of this passage.
The presentation of philosophical ideas step by step in a logical
form is itself known as *frequentatio*. The diction and elevated
rhetorical style of the opening quickly gives way to a more
urgently personal and familiar tone which reminds one of
Hopkins's:

> Thou art indeed just, Lord, if I contend
> With thee; but, sir, so what I plead is just.

Immediately we have the second reference to the black rocks which were first mentioned only five lines before the start of the apostrophe. The urgency of the appeal is dramatically emphasized by the alliterative force and the repetitive reference to the 'grisly feendly rokkes blake' and by the withholding to the end of the sentence of the *interrogatio* 'Why han ye wroght this werk unresonable?'

Dorigen admonishes God for creating the evil rocks and then, using the rhetorical vocabulary of the medieval logicians ('argumentz', 'causes', 'conclusion') concludes her own case by jibing at the defence of God's action that will be made by the learned clerks; and so the apostrophe ends with great feminine simplicity ('To clerkes lete I al disputison') which cannot fail in arousing our sympathy, with a final reference to the black rocks in which their evil nature, contrasting with the opening reference to God's 'purveiance', is emphasized by the slower movement of the verse to the Dantesque:

> 'But wolde God that alle thise rokkes blake
> Were sonken into helle for his sake!'
>   (891–2)

With her phobia for the rocks it is not surprising that Dorigen should make their removal the condition for her compliance with Aurelius's request that she should become his mistress. We hear much of the external qualities of this marriage but inevitably we can only conjecture at the kind of physical relationship which Dorigen and Arveragus enjoyed in the two years of their marriage before the latter's departure overseas. Whereas Dorigen is capable of great intensity of feeling as the apostrophe to God has shown, we are given little indication of her husband's emotional behaviour; he shows considerable human kindness in understanding Dorigen's predicament when Aurelius has successfully fulfilled his condition, but his strongest concern then, as always, is for the material effects upon his own reputation.

Before she makes her plea to God, Dorigen's friends try to take advantage of the lessening of her sorrow and attempt to comfort her: 'Awey to dryve hire derke fantasye'. The black rocks symbolize an apparent anomaly in the natural order of things, but, in a Freudian sense, the same symbolic black rocks with the additional suggestiveness of the water which surrounds

them, may also stand for the dark fantasy of Dorigen's mental anxiety that, in spite of her better judgement, she might be unfaithful to her husband. This is before Aurelius comes into her life; and, when he does, she modifies her rejection of his proposal immediately after she has made it. The human psychological problem created by the Sir Jasper Fidgets of society, however loyal, who leave their wives, however devoted, and go away from home to enhance their worldly status and to advance their business interests in the power game of life is a very real one.

We may be left in some doubt about Arveragus's temperament, but Chaucer does not stint his portrayal of his rival Aurelius who is now introduced as the typical Courtly Lover:

> Oon of the beste farynge man on lyve;
> Yong, strong, right vertuous, and riche, and wys . . .
>
> (932-3)

He goes through all the conventional pangs of unrequited love and throws himself at Dorigen's feet with 'Have mercy, sweete, or ye wol do me deye!' Dorigen refuses him saying 'I wol been his to whom that I am knyt'.

> But after that in pley thus seyde she:
> 'Aurelie,' quod she, 'by heighe God above,
> Yet wolde I graunte yow to been youre love,
> Syn I yow se so pitously complayne.
> Looke what day that endelong Britayne
> Ye remoeve alle the rokkes, stoon by stoon,
> That they ne lette ship ne boot to goon,—
> I seye, whan ye han maad the coost so clene
> Of rokkes that ther nys no stoon ysene,
> Thanne wol I love yow best of any man,
> Have heer my trouthe, in al that evere I kan'.
>
> (988-98)

Elsewhere in the story Dorigen reveals herself as a rather pathetic person dependant upon others in a crisis, and this softening of her refusal is a further indication that she is infirm of purpose as well as possessing a warm heart for members of the opposite sex. After all, she is able to make this jest ('in pley') in the midst of all her grief and professed avowals of love for her husband.

This indiscreet promise to Aurelius is, of course, the central feature of the whole of 'The Franklin's Tale'; it introduces an

element of suspense and without it there would be no story. Inevitably the rocks are again mentioned and here they assume yet another symbolic meaning. We have seen how they were a symbol of the power of nature to imperil her husband's safety, and that they also symbolized Dorigen's fear for her own possible infidelity; but now, and this is another of the Tale's paradoxes, they betoken the rock-fast permanency and enduring quality of her love for Arveragus. In her childlike innocency Dorigen has laid down the apparently impossible condition and now it is Aurelius who becomes the central character as he attempts to carry out his task. He first has recourse to prayer and his plea to Apollo loudly echoes Dorigen's own apostrophe to God, but in Aurelius's appeal it is noticeable that there is not the same repetitive insistence upon the rocks themselves.

In the Middle Ages the universe was an integral part of existence; it served as both calendar and clock and touched human life even more intimately through the belief in the influence of the planets upon the temperament and physical well-being of individuals. Every educated person was more familiar with its working than is the case today; but Chaucer's familiarity with the Ptolemaic system is evident in so much of his writing; for his 'litel sone Lewis' he wrote the instructional manual *Treatise on the Astrolabe*. As the planets in due order revolved around the earth at the centre, they were viewed against the backcloth of the fixed stars. Thus it was apparent that the sun took a year to complete its circular passage and the moon only a month. The reason for this which neither the Franklin, nor even Chaucer himself knew was that the earth was also moving round the sun at the same time. Anyway, the Franklin was prompted to appeal to Apollo to intercede tactfully on his behalf with Apollo's sister Lucena and: 'Preye hire she go no faster cours than ye . . .' (1066) because he knew that it was the moon that governs the tides and that when the sun and the moon were 'in opposition', directly opposite each other, at the full moon, then the spring tides would be at their highest. The Franklin had calculated that at high tide the water must be five fathoms above the top of the rocks if they were also to remain covered at low tide. The miracle, of course, could not be performed because the Franklin did not appreciate, although Chaucer would have known this himself, that even if the sun and moon were at

180 degrees to each other they would still both be travelling round the earth and would naturally affect the spring tides in different parts of the world and not only on the coast of Brittany.

We have noticed how Arveragus and Dorigen tried to reconcile in their relationship both the ideals of Courtly Love and those of Christian marriage, so also is there a similar fusion in the Tale of the accepted scientific principles of the day and the 'supersticious cursednesse' of magic about which the Franklin makes a special point of saying:

> For hooly chirches feith in oure bileve
> Ne suffreth noon illusioun us to greve.
>
> (1133–4)

But it is to *magyk natureel*, not the evil of black magic, to which Aurelius with his brother's help now turns when pure science has failed to achieve the desired result. 'I ne kan no termes of astrologye', says the Franklin as he intervenes in the description of the magical methods used by the Clerk, but he goes on to include an impressive array of the technical vocabulary used by the medieval astrologists with their Toledo Tables to calculate the positions of the planets, and which were:

> Ful wel corrected, ne ther lakked nought,
> Neither his *collect* ne his *expans yeeris*,
> Ne his *rootes*, ne his othere geeris,
> As been his *centris* and his *argumentz*
> And his *proporcioneles convenientz*
> For his *equacions* in every thyng.
>
> (1274–9)

It is easy enough in the light of this precise knowledge to dismiss the Franklin's apologetic remark as being as irrelevant as his similar apology for his lack of an understanding of rhetoric, but Professor Hodgson, shirking no difficulty, considers the passage in absorbing detail and concludes: 'We are clearly justified in assuming that Chaucer intended this long string of abstruse allusions to be vague and bewildering. This passage certainly does not seem to be a repetition of a favourite joke.'[9]

The important thing is that in the end,

> . . . thurgh his magik, for a wyke or tweye,
> It semed that alle the rokkes were aweye.
>
> (1295–6)

And with a certain amount of 'willing suspension of disbelief' the reader is convinced. Anyway, considerable suspense has been built up and we are keenly anticipatory of the effect of the miracle upon the other characters. Dorigen's apparently innocent and inocuous remark spoken in jest to Aurelius has placed her in an awkward dilemma; but what of Aurelius? How will he repay the Clerk's fee? Will he in turn demand his 'pound of flesh'? How will Arveragus react?

The Clerk of Orleans, the agent for all this magic, is the least obtrusive of all the participants in the drama but he is, nevertheless, an all-important figure at the very centre of the action. He is a skilfully depicted character and aptly called 'subtil'. With the introduction of the Clerk the narrative itself takes a more subtle turn and there is a liveliness that has been lacking hitherto with the conventional attitudes of Dorigen, Arveragus and Aurelius depicted one after the other. Now we have an 'outsider' brought into the story, a change from the three noble, courtly characters. With typical Chaucerian economy of description the scene shifts geographically, and a note of commerce is introduced. From the first the Clerk displays his skill: he greets Aurelius and his brother in Latin and tells them that he knows the cause of their journey before they themselves have time to explain it. He takes them to his house which, like the Franklin's own home, 'lakked no vitaille that myghte hem plese'. Then follows the conventionally impressive passing show of illusory magic such as Marlowe's Dr Faustus was treated to, and as with Dr Faustus, so with Aurelius, the last display is of an erotic nature in which he ironically imagines he is enjoying the charms of Dorigen.

After this very effective sample of the Clerk's abilities as a magician, he continues to impress as a forceful personality, a man of some standing who employs an efficient servant, who knows how to entertain and who can bring in a touch of humour. The domestic note is emphasized by a homeliness of dialogue not found elsewhere in the Tale:

> To hym this maister called his squier,
> And seyde hym thus: 'Is redy oure soper?
> Almoost an houre it is, I undertake,
> Sith I yow bad oure soper for to make,
> Whan that thise worthy men wenten with me
> Into my studie, ther as my bookes be.'

'Sire,' quod this squier, 'whan it liketh yow,
It is al redy, though ye wol right now.'
'Go we thanne soupe,' quod he, 'as for the beste.
Thise amorous folk somtyme moote han hir reste.'
(1209–18)

But after supper, four lines later, comes the bombshell:

He made it straunge, and swoor, so God hym save,
Lasse than a thousand pound he wolde nat have,
Ne gladly for that somme he wolde nat goon.
(1223–5)

However, Aurelius agrees: 'Ye shal be payed trewely, by my
trouthe!' and they set off on the return journey to Brittany.

And this was, as thise bookes me remembre,
The colde, frosty seson of Decembre.
　　Phebus wax old, and hewed lyk laton,
That in his hoote declynacion
Shoon as the burned gold with stremes brighte;
But now in Capricorn adoun he lighte,
Where as he shoon ful pale, I dar wel seyn.
The bittre frostes, with the sleet and reyn,
Destroyed hath the grene in every yerd.
Janus sit by the fyr, with double berd,
And drynketh of his bugle horn the wyn;
Biforn hym stant brawen of the tusked swyn,
And 'Nowel' crieth every lusty man.
(1243–55)

We have noticed how in order to give some degree of realism to
the Tale Chaucer has been at pains to give details of established
fact; here, at the start of the Clerk's magical operations, an air of
authority is provided by the conventional reference to 'thise
bookes' and a precise date of the operation is given in the conventionally decorative rhetorical manner by referring to the
sun's passage through the Zodiac. This also helps to prepare the
way for the astrological calculations which the Clerk is about to
make. This passage contains some of the finest poetry of the
Tale; the alliterative simile with the variation of the rhyme
pattern by confining the rhyme to the final syllable of 'laton'
and 'declynacion' leads into the bold alliterative line of 'Shoon
as the burned gold with stremes brighte', with its long flowing

vowel sounds contrasting with the short, clipped vowels describing the winter scene. The whole Tale is full of contrasts.
The characters of Arveragus and Aurelius, for instance, although
they shared a common interest in Dorigen, are very different;
the bustling, forceful,

> Arveragus, with heele and greet honour,
> As he that was of chivalrie the flour . . .
>
> (1087–8)

is compared to the more impulsive and insipid personality of 'the
sike Aurelius'. The tranquility of the 'gardyn ful of leves and of
floures', is contrasted with the storm-lashed 'grisly feendly
rokkes blake'. So here, not only is the summer compared to the
winter, but also the outdoors scene of 'bittre frostes' with the
'sleet and reyn' which 'destroyed hath the grene' is contrasted
with the homely warmth and robust Yule-tide good cheer of
Janus and his lusty companions as they are plied with food and
drink. A. C. Spearing considers that the double-bearded Janus
is a central image in the Tale, 'and he might be taken to stand
for the Franklin, offering a double perspective on the con-
vincingly human world of his Tale'.[10]

Much of Chaucer's skill as a story-teller derives from his
adroit handling of the part played by the narrator. In *Troilus and
Criseyde* where the narrator fills a variety of roles the poet made
it quite clear how important he considered the function of the
teller of the story to be, and in 'The Franklin's Tale' the Franklin
himself, as narrator, plays a very significant part, giving Chaucer
another means of providing a certain degree of objectivity and
also realism to the Tale. 'It is not surprising,' writes Nevill
Coghill, 'that Chaucer came to adopt the ambush of a double-
persona when he came to write the *Canterbury Tales*, for there
was much that he wished, or might wish, to say obliquely.'[11]

There is no doubt that Chaucer frequently used this ambush
to admonish his audience, but in 'The Franklin's Tale' we have
noticed the ambiguous Janus-like stand that he takes over
Courtly Love and Christian marriage, and over science and
magic, with his care not to offend against Christian teaching:

> For hooly chirches feith in oure bileve
> Ne suffreth noon illusioun us to greve.
>
> (1133–4)

Nevertheless, the Franklin as narrator is entirely convincing. I have already mentioned the suitability of the Tale to its teller; if the characters are themselves sometimes merely the stock idealistic portraits of convention, this cannot be said of the Franklin himself, who is very decidedly an individual. Chaucer stresses this in the General Prologue, in the interchanges between the Host and the Franklin, and in the many and varied comments he makes in the course of his Tale. In showing how the dramatic impulse to the telling of the Tale in the first place stems from the circumstances, the situation, and the interplay of the pilgrims themselves, Professor Kittredge says of the Franklin that 'he is speaking under the immediate influence of his admiration for the Squire and of his sense of the inferiority of his own son'.[12] And this is yet another way in which the poet imparts a degree of realism to his story. We have been given the picture, not of some colourless moralist, but of a real person, with a father's concern for his child and with all the human failings of class consciousness and a fondness for worldly pleasures and self-indulgence. This is what makes the Franklin convincing and which prevents Chaucer from appearing too much in evidence himself for, as G. T. Shepherd says:

> the Narrator must maintain throughout something of that initial *naiveté*, lest he be held responsible for the calamity. The poet cannot make a moral too emphatically, so the Narrator cannot be seen to identify himself too steadily with the logic of the destinies involved, or pass too magisterial a judgment on the actors who suffer them.[13]

Lest his audience should find Arveragus's insistence that Dorigen should keep her promise to be too unacceptable ethically or merely too far-fetched, the Franklin himself interrupts with:

> Paraventure an heep of yow, ywis,
> Wol holden hym a lewed man in this
> That he wol putte his wyf in jupartie.
> Herkneth the tale er ye upon hire crie.
> She may have bettre fortune than yow semeth;
> And whan that ye han herd the tale, demeth.
> (1493-8)

And what of our own judgement of the Tale and especially its ending with the narrator's final question to the audience,

> Lordynges, this question, thanne, wolde I aske now,
> Which was the mooste fre, as thynketh yow?
>
> (1621–2)

This question, another reminder of the oral tradition when a story was intended to stimulate further discussion amongst the listeners, is prompted by the reactions of each of the characters to the apparent removal of the rocks. First of all Dorigen in her dilemma confesses to her husband who replies that,

> 'Ye shul youre trouthe holden, by my fay!
> . . . Trouthe is the hyeste thyng that man may kepe:'
>
> (1474 and 1479)

and she goes off to her assignation in the garden with Aurelius. He, in his turn, has compassion on Dorigen's 'lamentacion' and is so impressed with Arveragus who 'so looth hym was his wyf sholde breke hir trouthe', and seeing such 'grete gentillesse' agrees to release her from her promise rather "Than ye to me sholde breke thus youre trouthe'. Aurelius now has his own dilemma to resolve. He determines to pay the Clerk's fee with a fifty per cent down payment in the hope that he will be allowed to pay off the balance of the debt by instalments spread over two or three years: 'My trouthe wol I kepe, I wol nat lye,' for 'I failled nevere of my trouthe as yit.' Aurelius tells the Clerk all about Arveragus's *gentillesse* which had prompted his own action in releasing Dorigen,

> 'And right as frely as he sente hire me,
> As frely sente I hire to hym ageyn.'
>
> (1604–5)

It is interesting in view of what we know about the Franklin himself that class-consciousness and professional status should be the considerations weighed by the Clerk when he too realizes that he must show generosity for:

> 'Everich of yow dide gentilly til oother.
> Thou art a squier, and he is a knyght;
> But God forbede, for his blisful myght,
> But if a clerk koude doon a gentil dede
> As wel as any of yow, it is no drede!'
>
> (1608–12)

And so all ends well with all the characters reconciled. The sanctity of marriage is upheld and, although Arveragus has, to be sure, imposed his *maistrie*, in doing so he implies that the non-Christian Courtly Love relationship has been rejected in the end. Nevertheless, as Nevill Coghill says, 'how to be happy though married is not its true theme. The true theme is noble behaviour.'[14] By noble behaviour he means *gentillesse*. Together with the marriage theme, so the theme of *gentillesse* has now been logically worked out; but implicit in this idea of *gentillesse* is the concept of *trouthe*, which is another of the Tale's dominant themes emphasized here by Arveragus and Aurelius in showing their final generosity. It is perhaps significant that the Clerk does not use the word *trouthe* in this context; he does use it when he says that he will insist on the full payment of his fee.

The legalistic overtones in the insistence of pledges and the maintenance of *trouthe* is in accord with the portrait of the Franklin, but here is yet another of the Tale's paradoxes. One would have thought that Arveragus, man of the world that he was, would have argued that Dorigen's first vow to be his humble 'trewe wyf' ('Have heer my trouthe, til that myn herte breste') was more legally binding than her later vow made in jest to Aurelius. Nevertheless, although we may find difficulty in sympathizing with his attitude, Arveragus surely fulfils most completely the ideal of *gentillesse*. The Franklin warns us at the beginning that,

> Ire, siknesse, or constellacioun,
> Wyn, wo, or chaungynge of complexioun
> Causeth ful ofte to doon amys or speken.
>   (781–3)

But even so, the more flamboyant Aurelius with all his 'wo' and love-sickness is not nearly such an integrated personality, and the Clerk, with his much more mercenary outlook, puts himself out of the running as a serious contender for the title of 'mooste fre'. The weaknesses of Aurelius and the Clerk serve to highlight the ideals of marriage, *gentillesse* and *trouthe* as they are revealed in the harmonious relationship between Arveragus and Dorigen. It is this maintenance of such a delicate balance between its many varied aspects that is one of the most striking features of the Tale. There is just sufficient realism to make the moral solution credible, and the difficult middle road is taken between

the purely tragic (which the story so nearly becomes) and the right balance is struck between the worlds of courtly society, Armorik Brittany, commercial Orleans and the land of Faerie.

'If a story is to be judged by the taste it leaves, none is more satisfying than "The Franklin's Tale".'[15] All the ingredients of a good story are here, but it is Chaucer's narrative skill in the blending of these ingredients that provides the flavour.

The Pardoner's Tale

Elde the hore, he was in the vawwarde,
And bar the baner bifore Deth—bi riht he hit claymede.
Kynde cam aftur hym, with many kyne sores,
As pokkes and pestilences, and moche peple shente;
So Kynde thorw corupcions kulde ful mony.
Deth cam dryvyng aftur and al to duste paschte
Kynges and knyhtes, caysers and popes.
Lered ne lewed he lefte no man stande;
That he hitte evene, nevere stured aftur.

(Langland: *Piers Plowman*. C Text:
Passus XXIII, lines 220–8)

During the last centuries of the Middle Ages there arose a deep and macabre obsession with death. In *The Waning of the Middle Ages*, J. Huizinga points out how all-pervasive was the primitive and terrifying image of death which intensified as so much of the structure of medieval life began to crumble:

> No other epoch has laid so much stress as the expiring Middle Ages on the thought of death. An everlasting call of *memento mori* resounds through life. Denis the Carthusian, in his *Directory of the Life of Nobles*, exhorts them: 'And when going to bed at night, he should consider how, just as he now lies down himself, soon strange hands will lay his body in the grave.'[1]

The conception of death was crude and direct. It had to be, since so much of the complex thought of earlier centuries was entirely unsuited to the unsophisticated techniques of forms like the sermon and the popular woodcut, media through which the idea of death was communicated. And it is because the images are so direct and primitive that the vision had such an impact on medieval life. In the late Middle Ages, the elegiac approach of lamentation for the passing of former glories diminished in importance. Instead, attention focused more and more on the motif of physical decay of the human body. Terrifying visual representation of the spectacle of decomposition was frequent in tomb carvings and paintings. This we may find in the horrific images in the churchyard of the Innocents at Paris, for example, and in the poetry of François Villon. Also represented pictorially in woodcuts, sculpture, frescoes and other forms was a third idea, the Dance of Death. The force of this image lay in the identification of living men with the inevitable fact of death, for the vision was of an actual dancing *body* carrying off men; the image did not become a skeleton until late in the fifteenth century with Holbein's 'Dance of Death'. These ideas, which were widely expressed in art and literature, used and increased medieval man's fear of death. The church in turn played upon the obsession and used it to further moral arguments. And so we find that the vision of death occupies a major place in medieval sermons.

The obsessive vision of death took on a new and terrible aspect in the late summer of 1348, when the Black Death reached the southern ports of England and began to ravage the land and its people. Throughout the year, the rat-born bubonic plague had been spreading swiftly through Europe from the Black Sea, leaving in its wake a trail of desolation. In England the first epidemic alone carried off at least one third of the population, and all grew to fear the sinister symptoms of infection, the black boils and delirious agony. Here, it seemed, was a Dance of Death which would only end with the total destruction of mankind. And so, just as Wulfstan, centuries before, had attributed the widespread ravages of Danish invasions to the moral decline of English society,[2] now the plague took on the aspect of an apocalyptic sign, interpreted by many as a token of God's wrath and vengeance on a sinful people.

Yet the moral exhortations of the religious failed to halt the pestilence. The church itself, in fact, became one of the chief victims of the social and economic collapse consequent on the plague. Many religious houses lost all their wealth, and the Black Death carried off the very men needed for their reconstruction. The life of common men was affected even more, as harvests rotted unreaped in the fields around empty villages, and cattle wandered untended and dying of murrain. G. G. Coulton sums up the situation when he writes: 'The Black Death . . . shook many things to the very base, and overthrew those whose foundations were faulty, while the sounder survived.'[3] Medieval life was totally disrupted, and the religious and social structure of England largely collapsed.

It is against this background that we must set the tale of death and damnation which the Pardoner tells to the Canterbury pilgrims. The Pardoner is the last of the pilgrims to be described in 'The General Prologue'. Like the Summoner, with whom he rides as a close companion, the Pardoner is given a full and detailed portrait:

> With hym ther rood a gentil PARDONER
> Of Rouncivale, his freend and his compeer,
> That streight was comen fro the court of Rome.
> Ful loude he soong 'Com hider, love, to me!'
>   (669–72)

They are singing together a love-song, something which immediately strikes a note discordant with their ecclesiastical situations. This sense of incongruity grows stronger as the description proceeds. The Pardoner follows the latest trends in fashion, or so he thinks: 'Hym thoughte he rood al of the newe jet' (682), and his deliberate jauntiness associates him with the secular life. He is further distanced from his calling by his appearance. He is physically repugnant, although he does not have the openly frightening appearance of the Summoner. Yet there is something more subtly repulsive about the Pardoner. His appearance is effeminate, with long fair hair and staring eyes:

> This Pardoner hadde heer as yelow as wex,
> But smothe it heeng as dooth a strike of flex;
> By ounces henge his lokkes that he hadde,
> And therwith he his shuldres overspradde;
> But thynne it lay, by colpons oon and oon . . .
> Swiche glarynge eyen hadde he as an hare.
>
> (675–9, 684)

His soft, high-pitched, bleating voice and his smooth complexion emphasize this, and Chaucer sums up the total effect with an image of sexual impotence taken from the rural scene:

> A voys he hadde as smal as hath a goot.
> No berd hadde he, ne nevere sholde have;
> As smothe it was as it were late shave.
> I trowe he were a geldyng or a mare.
>
> (688–91)

These features show clearly that Chaucer's Pardoner is an eunuch, and we owe to Professor W. C. Curry the realization that Chaucer must have been very familiar with medieval physiognomy literature (which contained elaborate character judgements in accordance with a man's features and bodily form), for the Pardoner's physical characteristics are those of the medieval type of *eunuchus ex nativitate*.[4] The very type itself intensifies our feeling of disgust at the sight of the Pardoner.

The second part of Chaucer's introductory description of the Pardoner concerns his activities in his office. This forms a striking parallel with the previous details of his physical characteristics, for here again there is a strong sense of delusion and emptiness. Physically the Pardoner is not what he seems. His hair may

be fair and long, but it is thin and matted, and his attempt to follow fashion in his clothing is a mockery. His attitude to his ecclesiastical position is similar, since it is based wholly on deceit and hypocrisy. Poor, ignorant folk who take advantage of his services merely fill his pockets with their hard-earned savings, and, of course, he has no interest at all in their spiritual welfare:

> But with thise relikes, whan that he fond
> A povre person dwellynge upon lond,
> Upon a day he gat hym moore moneye
> Than that the person gat in monthes tweye . . .
>   (701–4)

There is an insidious and sinister evil in the Pardoner which Chaucer clearly conveys in this initial portrait, and yet, at the same time, we are aware of another side to our attitude to the rogue. For he is also a figure of high comedy. This is the effect of Chaucer's summary of his valueless relics:

> He hadde a croys of latoun ful of stones,
> And in a glas he hadde pigges bones.
>   (699–700)

And it is the note on which the description ends, as we are given a glimpse of his skilful technique in church.

From the outset, then, Chaucer calls forth from us a dual response to his Pardoner. He is at once a figure of comedy and of sinister evil. This is a fundamental feature of Chaucer's design, for it produces a character who is both a type and a full and rounded personality. A type Chaucer's Pardoner certainly is, but not, of course, of the ideal *quaestor* or pardoner appointed by the church whose task was to receive payment from a sinner in place of penance. By the fourteenth century false pardoners similar to Chaucer's character could be found throughout England. There is a great deal of evidence to support this, not only in historical documents, but also in works of literature such as the satirical description of a pardoner in William Langland's *Piers Plowman*.[5] So Chaucer has not drawn an exaggerated picture of an unreal villain. On the contrary, both he and his contemporaries must have been very familiar with such manifestations of the widespread corruption of the church in the later Middle Ages.

Although he briefly interrupts the Wife of Bath with a blatant but amusing lie,[6] the Pardoner does not hold the stage again until he is invited by Harry Bailly to dispel the gloom created by the Physician's Tale of false justice and cruel murder. Harry Bailly clearly wants a bawdy *fabliau* story, and the Pardoner, despite his ecclesiastical office, appears to be quite ready to oblige. But he is forestalled by the 'gentils', who demand a more constructive and 'honest' Tale:

> 'Nay, lat hym telle us of no ribaudye!
> Telle us som moral thyng, that we may leere
> Som wit, and thanne wol we gladly heere.'
>
> (324–6)

To this the Pardoner readily agrees, and, provided with a glass of ale and a cake, he proceeds with his Prologue.

The opening lines set the tone of the Prologue and Tale:

> 'Lordynges,' quod he, 'in chirches whan I preche,
> I peyne me to han an hauteyn speche,
> And rynge it out as round as gooth a belle,
> For I kan al by rote that I telle.
> My theme is alwey oon, and evere was—
> *Radix malorum est Cupiditas.*'
>
> (329–34)

From the start we see the Pardoner as a preacher, and we are at once reminded of the concluding lines of his portrait in 'The General Prologue'. Preaching he loves, and it is an art in which he is highly skilled. In these opening lines the compelling drama of his style is conveyed through the urgent rhythm of the verse, and we are immediately captivated by his roguish boasting and self-confidence. It is a technique which he has used to his own advantage for many years, successfully manipulating his unfortunate congregations to fill his pockets. Preaching, however, was the task of the priest, and not of lay officers of the church. Lay pardoners were therefore not permitted to preach. Yet Chaucer's Pardoner appears to be a layman, and so his whole position is illegal. But the church's legislation concerning such activities was ineffectual. In addition to preaching it attempted to exercise some sort of control over the practice of selling pardons by issuing licences to its appointed officers. Chaucer's Pardoner possesses such a licence, and he tells the pilgrims that

he shows this official permit wherever he preaches in order to establish his authority:

> 'First I pronounce whennes that I come,
> And thanne my bulles shewe I, alle and some.
> Oure lige lordes seel on my patente,
> That shewe I first, my body to warente,
> That no man be so boold, ne preest ne clerk,
> Me to destourbe of Cristes hooly werk.'
>
> (335–40)

But the Pardoner is not content with this bishop's seal alone. He has a variety of other documents, probably forged, which he uses to deceive his congregation:

> 'Bulles of popes and of cardynales,
> Of patriarkes and bishopes I shewe . . .'
>
> (342–3)

Right from the start, the Pardoner is carried away by the sound of his own voice and the thought of his skill and success. Chaucer creates this very real enthusiasm in the fast-flowing rhythm of the verse, and in the highly appropriate cooking image:

> 'And in Latyn I speke a wordes fewe,
> To saffron with my predicacioun,
> And for to stire hem to devocioun.'
>
> (344–6)

With the word 'devocioun' we might expect the Pardoner to turn to his official task as dispenser of pardons, but Chaucer's character has more entertainment to offer. He turns now to the bones and pieces of cloth which he carries in glass containers, holy relics with beneficial powers. That they are useless fakes the Pardoner knows full well, and he confesses this with subtle irony to his audience when he says: 'Relikes been they, as wenen they echoon' (349). The Pardoner has nothing but contempt for the poor, ignorant souls who are completely taken in by his practices, although these are the people who provide him with a living.

At this point in his Prologue, the Pardoner's technique changes. His reported reminiscence imperceptibly gives way to direct speech in line 352. This passage the Pardoner has lifted bodily from a sermon to country folk, and its directness and immediacy introduces a new dimension into the address. The effect

of this change of technique is that the pilgrims now become the Pardoner's congregation. Ironically, only two lines previously, as we have seen, the Pardoner has derided his congregation, and now it is not only each of the pilgrims but also we, the listeners, who are the objects of his contempt. Yet we continue to be fascinated by the spectacle of dramatic self-revelation, and our interest never leaves this villain as he confesses his whole technique to us.

The Pardoner attributes both physical and psychological properties to his relics, and Chaucer's easy objective style invites us to accept the Pardoner's claims on their face value. Within the verse, however, there runs a subtle tone of qualification. It is all too good to be true. The Pardoner's over-simplification is conveyed in the swift movement and alliteration of 'Wol every wyke, er that the cok hym croweth' (362), and the blatant improbability of the power to cure jealousy converts the whole passage into an entertainment for the pilgrims. This is most clear in the satire on the immorality of priests:

> 'And nevere shal he moore his wyf mystriste,
> Though he the soothe of hir defaute wiste,
> Al had she taken prestes two or thre.'
>
> (369–71)

The sexual thread is taken up again in the last paragraph of direct quotation from a sermon:

> 'Goode men and wommen, o thyng warne I yow:
> If any wight be in this chirche now
> That hath doon synne horrible, that he
> Dar nat, for shame, of it yshryven be,
> Or any womman, be she yong or old,
> That hath ymaad hir housbonde cokewold,
> Swich folk shal have no power ne no grace
> To offren to my relikes in this place.'
>
> (377–84)

Here we become aware for the first time of the Pardoner's obsession with sin, an obsession which is clarified and made more emphatic as the Tale proceeds. He is fascinated by sin and, as will be seen, his Tale becomes an exploration of the idea of mortal sin which leads to death and damnation. The apparent sincerity of the Pardoner's warning to those in mortal sin is clearly quite out of character. Like all the devices he employs,

it has a calculated purpose, for it implies that all who fail to come
forward are guilty of such sin, and none will wish to be placed in
this position before the eyes of his neighbours.

When the Pardoner returns from direct quotation to his confessional conversation, his hypocrisy becomes more explicit.
Ironically, he is guilty of the very sin against which he preaches:

> 'Of avarice and of swich cursednesse
> Is al my prechyng, for to make hem free
> To yeven hir pens, and namely unto me.
> For myn entente is nat but for to wynne,
> And nothyng for correccioun of synne.'
>
> (400–4)

There can be no question of self-deception here. He knows that
he is a hypocrite, but there is no hint of shame. He takes great
pride in his skill as preacher and showman, and the measure of
his success lies in his material gains—a hundred marks a year.
Throughout this section of his Prologue, the Pardoner's skill
and enthusiasm is conveyed through the fast rhythm of the verse
and, more especially, through the dramatic realism of the imagery
which is drawn from the immediate experience of the countryside and rural life. There is, first, the delightful parallel of the
Pardoner's long neck in the pulpit with a dove sitting on a barn.
Then, as the confession continues and we become more aware
of the Pardoner's total corruption, there is a more sombre thought
in the image of the damned souls who go black-berrying. Finally,
this suggestion becomes darker and more sinister in the repeated
image of the snake:

> 'Thanne wol I stynge hym with my tonge smerte
> In prechyng, so that he shall nat asterte . . .'
>
> (413–14)

and

> 'Thus spitte I out my venym under hewe
> Of hoolynesse, to semen hooly and trewe.'
>
> (421–2)

It is but a short step from here to the story of Eden and the Fall
of Man, an association of real significance in the Middle Ages,
particularly among a company of pilgrims.

The climax of the Pardoner's Prologue takes the form of a
summary of his motives and techniques:

'But shortly myn entente I wol devyse:
I preche of no thyng but for coveityse.
Therfore my theme is yet, and evere was,
Radix malorum est Cupiditas.
Thus kan I preche agayn that same vice
Which that I use, and that is avarice.
But though myself be gilty in that synne,
Yet kan I maken oother folk to twynne
From avarice, and soore to repente.
But that is nat my principal entente;
I preche nothyng but for coveitise.
Of this mateere it oghte ynogh suffise.'

(423–34)

The hypocrisy of his whole approach is more explicit than ever here. And the whole sequence is masterly in its irony, for the Pardoner's rhetorical skill in preaching is so great that he actually succeeds in turning his congregation from the vice which he himself pursues. This is the final paradox. His preaching is obviously much more compelling than that of the good Parson, and yet the repentance of his congregation is not the Pardoner's primary aim. His preaching is directed towards material gain, and it is this idea which he expands with emphasis at the conclusion of his Prologue. The repetition of the phrase 'I wol' and the fast rhythm produce a strong assertive tone. The Pardoner will allow nothing to stand in his way. Chaucer has again taken the details from everyday country life, and we are close to the reality of poverty and social distress which Chaucer approaches here and elsewhere in the *Canterbury Tales* with deep compassion.

The Pardoner's Prologue takes the form of a confession, a deliberate revelation of motives and techniques. This device was a common convention in medieval literature, and we find it, for example, in the *Roman de la Rose* in the confession of False Seeming. It is also the device which Chaucer employs with such skill in the Wife of Bath's Prologue to her Tale. It is important to recognize that this conventional framework lies behind Chaucer's approach. It is, at the same time, highly appropriate to the Pardoner whose self-confident pride demands an outlet of confessional exhibitionism. There is, of course, much more to the Pardoner's Prologue than a simple medieval convention. Chaucer has combined with this a wealth of realistic detail, and

he has presented the whole structure through fast-moving dramatic speech which forces us to listen to the performer. Such a man as the Pardoner must of necessity boast of his skill and gloat over the misfortunes of his unfortunate victims. And indeed he does so with such vigour that we are completely absorbed by the spectacle. We may wish at times to rise up in indignation and pass moral censure on the villain, but at the same time we are prevented by his hypnotic power. We are taken into his confidence and experience a sense of exhilaration, just as we do when we share the thoughts of Macbeth or Iago. The Pardoner acts out his own wickedness in an orgy of self-dramatization which we, the audience, cannot resist.

The Pardoner begins his Tale with a detailed account of the sins indulged by the young men of Flanders. The description is realistic in its technique, for we have a striking picture of the gamblers and dancing-girls, of the strident noise and whirling movements. Yet there is more to this scene-setting than would appear at first sight. The whole description is coloured by the personality of the Pardoner. He betrays a certain fascination for the horrors of the immorality with which he is concerned, although this is clearly accompanied by a tone of moral indignation. This fascination is conveyed through the accuracy and immediacy of the details of the account; there is, for example, the piling up of information in lists:

> As riot, hasard, stywes, and tavernes,
> Where as with harpes, lutes, and gyternes,
> They daunce and pleyen at dees bothe day and nyght . . .
>
> (465–7)

and:

> And right anon thanne comen tombesteres
> Fetys and smale, and yonge frutesteres,
> Syngeres with harpes, baudes, wafereres . . .
>
> (477–9)

It is also recreated in the violence of the rhythm. We can hear his voice rising in pitch through the first eight lines until, with a gasping emphasis, the syntax brings him to a halt on the long, important words 'superfluytee abhomynable'. The tone of moral indignation which balances the Pardoner's interest in the details

of sin is found in the imagery of this opening verse paragraph. The idea that sin is a direct and active opposition to God is clearly expressed in the transformation of the tavern into a temple where the Devil is worshipped by the young sinners:

> And eten also and drynken over hir myght,
> Thurgh which they doon the devel sacrifise
> Withinne that develes temple, in cursed wise . . .
>
> (468-70)

This is followed by a more specific instance in the traditional medieval idea that swearing tore apart the body of Christ and crucified him again:

> Hir othes been so grete and so dampnable
> That it is grisly for to heere hem swere.
> Oure blissed Lordes body they totere,—
> Hem thoughte that Jewes rente hym noght ynough . . .
>
> (472-5)

Both these sins which the Pardoner discusses with such relish are forms of blasphemy. Swearing is clearly verbal blasphemy, and no less blasphemous is the worship of the devil in the tavern sins. Blasphemy is a major theme in the Tale, especially in the Sermon Digression, and the Pardoner considers it to be the worst of all sins:

> Lo, rather he forbedeth swich sweryng
> Than homycide or many a cursed thyng;
> I seye that, as by ordre, thus it stondeth . . .
>
> (643-5)

To say that blasphemy is a sin worse than murder because it comes earlier in the prohibitions of the Ten Commandments is typical of the imaginative way in which the Pardoner uses the Scriptures and ecclesiastical ideas. The idea has a special significance for the human comedy among the pilgrims, since this is a sly attack on Harry Bailly whose vigorously emotional response to 'The Physician's Tale' included many examples of blasphemous swearing:

> Oure Hooste gan to swere as he were wood;
> 'Harrow!' quod he, 'by nayles and by blood!'
>
> (287-8)

But the Pardoner's idea has a more important function than this.
Throughout his Tale he is concerned to show the interconnection between all sins. He is, of course, absorbed by the details
of individual sins, but his main purpose is to show how great
and terrifying is sin by fusing all sins together to produce a mag-
nification of evil. He begins to stress the interconnection of sins
at the beginning of the Sermon Digression:

> To kyndle and blowe the fyr of lecherye,
> That is annexed unto glotonye.
> The hooly writ take I to my witnesse
> That luxurie is in wyn and dronkenesse.
>
> (481–4)

Gluttony and lechery are closely related, a fact which the
Pardoner illustrates with two highly appropriate references. The
first is a reference to Saint Paul's Letter to Ephesians, although
Chaucer's medieval meaning of the word 'luxurie' is more specifically *sexual* excess, as opposed to Paul's more general meaning
(*luxuria*—excess). The second refers to the biblical story of Lot,
who was led to commit incestuous sin by excess of wine. Later
in the sermon gluttony is again fused with the greater sin of
blasphemy. Similarly, the Pardoner's attack on gambling begins
with a list of other sins which are closely interconnected:

> Hasard is verray mooder of lesynges,
> And of deceite, and cursed forswerynges,
> Blaspheme of Crist, manslaughtre, and wast also
> Of catel and of tyme . . .
>
> (591–4)

And the conclusion of the whole digression brings the various
sins together once again, and fuses them within the greater unity
of the idea of blasphemy:

> This fruyt cometh of the bicched bones two,
> Forsweryng, ire, falsnesse, homycide.
> Now, for the love of Crist, that for us dyde,
> Lete youre othes, bothe grete and smale.
>
> (656–9)

This, then, is the Pardoner's overall design in the Sermon
Digression. It provides unity within the variety of the sins and
illustrations in the homily and, more important, it serves to link

the digression with the actual Tale of the three revellers. Some commentators have seen little connection at all between the digression on sin and the Tale itself, but Chaucer has established a positive structural link. The revellers, who begin their quest for Death in a tavern, are guilty of all the sins which the Pardoner condemns in his sermon. In their Tale the fusion of the sins of gluttony, gambling and murder creates a larger evil similar in dimensions to the combined blasphemy of the sins of the homily. Their avarice is therefore magnified by its inclusion within a wider and darker vision of sin, blasphemy itself, and in this is to be found the true moral force of the Tale and its text of '*Radix malorum est Cupiditas*'.

The Sermon Digression is no less a masterpiece in its technical structure. As we have already seen in the Prologue to the Tale, the Pardoner prides himself on his skill as a preacher. The sermon set within the Tale clearly proves that this is no vain boast, for the Pardoner's histrionic powers are indeed commanding. It is not just a dramatic harangue, but it reveals an accomplished use of rhetoric and the devices of the sermon as a literary form. Just as there was an elaborate theory of poetry in the Middle Ages—the *ars poetica* which features, for example, in 'The Nun's Priest's Tale'—so a number of works were written on the art of preaching, the *ars praedicandi*. Much of our knowledge of this complex theory we gain from the scholarship of G. R. Owst,[7] and his studies show how closely the method and detailed devices used by the Pardoner connect with medieval sermon literature. Unlike the sermon presented by the Parson, the Pardoner's sermon makes use only of the technical devices of the preacher while largely ignoring the broader complexities of structure set down in the *artes praedicandi*. Basically, the structure was based on division of material into sets of three: the text was divided into three sections, each supported by additional biblical material; then these would be divided again. The whole structure was unified by rhetorical devices, especially *exempla*, which connected the various parts of the sermon. The *exempla* are illustrative stories or references of varying length (in fact, the whole tale of the three rioters is an extended *exemplum*), and although the Pardoner makes little use of the rules of structural form in the sermon, *exempla* and other devices are used to great effect. The text, correctly termed 'theme', is illustrated and

expanded by a number of *exempla* taken from the Bible and religious books, or from classical learning or folk lore and legend. As the Pardoner himself explains in his Prologue:

> 'Thanne telle I hem ensamples many oon
> Of olde stories longe tyme agoon.'
>
> (435–6)

To illustrate the evils of gluttony the Pardoner briefly reminds his audience of the biblical stories of Lot and Herod. The story of Eden and the Fall of Man he also attributes to the sin of gluttony in the eating of the forbidden fruit. From classical learning he takes the story of Attila as a warning to drunkards, and the sin of gambling he illustrates with stories of Stilboun and Demetrius. A varied effect is achieved by numerous references to religious teachers or classical authorities. In his argument against gluttony the Pardoner appeals to Seneca, the Latin stoic philosopher who enjoyed considerable popularity in the Middle Ages, and throughout his sermon he calls upon the evidence of biblical figures like Saint Paul, Matthew and Jeremiah. Such quotation from and reference to recognized authorities was a familiar device recommended in the theory of preaching. Clearly the Pardoner makes skilful use of his knowledge according to the methods of the *artes praedicandi*. In addition it is interesting to note that his references are accurate. Villain though he is, he is no fool, and he has learned his craft and its tools well.

He is equally skilful in the use of rhetorical devices which form part of the medieval theory of *ars poetica*.[8] The most notable of these is the device of *exclamatio* or *apostrophatio*. This technique is employed for the purpose of calling forth an emotional response from the audience, and the Pardoner first employs it when he relates the sin of gluttony to Adam's sin and the Fall of Man:

> O glotonye, ful of cursednesse!
> O cause first of oure confusioun!
> O original of oure dampnacioun,
> Til Crist hadde boght us with his blood agayn! . . .
> O glotonye, on thee wel oghte us pleyne!
>
> (498–501, 512)

He then expands this with a rhetorical lamentation of a conventional kind:

> Allas! the shorte throte, the tendre mouth,
> Maketh that est and west and north and south,
> In erthe, in eir, in water, men to swynke
> To gete a glotoun deyntee mete and drynke!
>
> (517–20)

This sequence follows quite closely the development of the verse
in 'The Nun's Priest's Tale' in the apostrophe and lamentation
which Chaucer includes when Chauntecleer is seized by the fox.
One other example of *exclamatio* in the Pardoner's sermon is
worthy of special note, for it combines rhetorical convention
with realism of a most forceful kind. It takes the form of an
apostrophe to the belly as the cause of all evil in men:

> O wombe! O bely! O stynkyng cod,
> Fulfilled of dong and of corrupcioun!
> At either ende of thee foul is the soun.
>
> (534–6)

The combination of convention and realism which we find here
is a crucial feature of the whole Sermon Digression. It is this
which makes the sermon itself so compelling and dramatic. The
Pardoner specifically describes gluttony in terms of food and
drink, and thus it becomes far more immediate than the mere
abstract concept would be. He talks of the details of cookery and
food, describing with relish the delights of the table, and un-
ashamedly revealing his preoccupation with the material things
of life. Realism comes to the fore in his remarkable portrait of
the drunkard:

> A lecherous thyng is wyn, and dronkenesse
> Is ful of stryvyng and of wrecchednesse.
> O dronke man, disfigured is thy face,
> Sour is thy breeth, foul artow to embrace,
> And thurgh thy dronke nose semeth the soun
> As though thou seydest ay 'Sampsoun, Sampsoun!'
> And yet, God woot, Sampsoun drank nevere no wyn.
> Thou fallest as it were a styked swyn;
> Thy tonge is lost, and al thyn honeste cure;
> For dronkenesse is verray sepulture
> Of mannes wit and his discrecioun.
>
> (549–59)

His aim here is primarily to entertain, to delight his audience
with his accurate description and to display his professional skill

as a preacher. Chaucer's descriptive method here is not to amass a list of details, but to select significant features of the drunkard and emphasize them alone. The rhetorical device of onomatopoeia is skilfully employed as the Pardoner approximates the drunkard's heavy breathing with the phrase 'Sampsoun, Sampsoun', and then a change of rhythm marks out the contrast with the biblical figure of Sampson: 'And yet, God woot, Sampsoun drank nevere no wyn' (555). Equally appropriate is the idea that wine kills careful judgement; and the image of the 'sepulture' takes on an additional interest of irony when we connect it with the lethal poison which the two revellers mistake for wine in the ensuing Tale. The Pardoner has further details with which to delight his audience, details which suggest a full knowledge of wine and the wine trade. He warns them of the dangers of 'the white wyn of Lepe':

> That is to selle in Fysshstrete or in Chepe.
> This wyn of Spaigne crepeth subtilly
> In othere wynes, growynge faste by,
> Of which ther ryseth swich fumositee
> That whan a man hath dronken draughtes thre,
> And weneth that he be at hoom in Chepe,
> He is in Spaigne, right at the toune of Lepe,—
>   (564–70)

The repetition of the 's' sound in the verse gives a striking sense of the creeping intoxication of the wine, and the whole passage is an imaginative *tour de force* of entertainment.

At this point the Pardoner turns back to his scholarly *exempla*, and calls his audience to attend closely to his wisdom: 'But herkneth, lordynges, o word, I yow preye' (573). The punctuation here breaks up the rhythm of the verse, and thus a more sombre tone is re-established after the exciting physical description of the drunkard. We never forget, however, that it is the Pardoner who is speaking; his personality is always present. In his enthusiasm, for example, having promised to refer to biblical *exempla*, he turns instead to classical history, to Attila. Similarly, his personal involvement is unmistakable in the amusing parenthesis: 'Nat Samuel, but Lamuel, seye I' (585). As the Pardoner proceeds to the sin of gambling we notice a further change in the rhythm. The opening lines are slow and matter-of-fact, but as he warms to his subject the verse speeds up and the lines become shorter and follow at a great pace:

> If that a prynce useth hasardrye,
> In alle governaunce and policye
> He is, as by commune opinioun,
> Yholde the lasse in reputacioun.
>
> (599–602)

The first illustration of the evils of gambling offers still more variety of technique. Chaucer presents this *exemplum* in the form of a short simple narrative. The story is quite self-contained, and it is brought alive by Chaucer's skilful use of dramatic speech and the three-fold repetition of Stilboun's refusal to form an alliance with Corinth.

The final section of the sermon concerns blasphemy. It is appropriate that this should conclude the homily since, as we have seen, it is this sin in which the Pardoner sums up the wickedness of all other sins. Again we find a combination of realism and convention in the style of this verse paragraph. The Pardoner adheres closely to medieval rhetorical technique when he clearly states his intentions at the outset:

> Now wol I speke of othes false and grete
> A word or two, as olde bookes trete.
>
> (629–30)

The 'olde bookes' and the scriptural *exempla* are also part of the medieval *ars praedicandi*. And the repetition of the word 'sweryng' is another rhetorical device. Alongside this, however, we find realistic speech in the examples of blasphemous swearing, the second of which, 'By his nayles', is a sly thrust at Harry Bailly. These examples the Pardoner relates to everyday life, and especially to gambling. Finally, death is linked with all this in the ironic epithet used to describe the dice: 'the bicched bones two'.

The Pardoner's sermon clearly operates, on one level, as a satire of contemporary preaching. But, as we have seen, this is not its primary aim. It is true that the Pardoner's skilful manipulation of so many recognized techniques of the *ars praedicandi* must produce a mock effect, but our attention is constantly focused on the speaker himself and his personality rather than the abstract idea of a sermon. For the sermon constitutes a further stage in the Pardoner's conscious self-dramatization and in the revelation of his character. Such is his power over those

who listen that it is impossible to escape. The effect is hypnotic. At the same time it is highly entertaining. The subject matter of the sermon is skilfully varied, and so too is his compelling style, with its combination of high rhetoric and low, coarse colloquialisms, of sombre biblical reference and the fast rhythms of exciting narrative. He is outstandingly successful as preacher and entertainer, and even if he cannot convince the wily Harry Bailly, there will be many other simple folk who will continue to be taken in by the villain's tricks and furnish him with his handsome annual income.

When at last we return to the Tale, the Pardoner plunges right into the heart of the story. It is of no consequence that the 'riotoures thre' have not been mentioned previously in the Tale. This sort of continuity is not important, and the Pardoner is obviously not aiming to provide a continuous logical thread. We have only to see how he jumps from one style to another and from one subject or *exemplum* to the next to realize this. To criticize Chaucer on the grounds that he is inconsistent is to misunderstand an important feature of the Pardoner's character. He is always master of his material, and he is prepared to use anything for his own ends, however illogical his transitions may be.

The language of the narrative itself is simple and the verse moves at a great pace. Chaucer's technique is marked by careful selection of details, such as the tinkling of the bell in the funeral procession, and at once we are present at the scene, and involved in the ensuing dialogue. Through the dramatic interplay of the characters in the dialogue we are given a clear picture of the revellers and the boy. By contrast to the former, there is no guile or pretence in the boy. His language is straightforward and colloquial:

> 'He was, pardee, an old felawe of youres;
> And sodeynly he was yslayn to-nyght,
> Fordronke, as he sat on his bench upright.'
>   (672–4)

And there is an open innocence in his final remark: 'Thus taughte me my dame; I sey namoore.' (684). Although the personification of death was a common device in medieval literature and art, the vivid imagery of the verse shows that the boy really does think of death in this way. It is as though he has

witnessed the very act of death cleaving with his spear the heart
of a comrade. The violent rhythms of the dialogue, punctuated
by blasphemous oaths, continue until the three rioters have
pledged themselves in brotherhood in their search for Death.
Just as he is a real person to the innocent boy, Death is no less
real to the revellers, who refer to him as a false traitor. And thus,
in accordance with the obsessive medieval vision of Death, it is
a real person whom they set out to find and kill. This brings
into the narrative the idea of a quest, which is a key feature
of the structure of the Tale. And it is the concrete reality of
Chaucer's adaptation of the conventional personification of death
which gives to the quest its drama and immediacy.

Eventually, of course, the revellers reach the end of their
quest, but the death they meet is not in the form of a person.
They do, however, meet a person during their search, the Old
Man who is engaged on the same quest for Death as they are.
Who is the Old Man in the Tale? There have been many answers
to this question. Some readers have seen the Old Man as an
allegory of Death itself, and at first sight there would appear to
be some truth in this view. Within the quest for the person of
Death, this figure is the sole person encountered by the revellers.
What is more, his closing remarks show quite clearly that he
knows a great deal about Death—even where he may be found.
In contrast to this, however, there is the basic incongruity that
the Old Man is himself engaged in a fruitless search for Death.
Chaucer must intend us to associate the Old Man with Death,
but a specific allegorical reading merely confuses the meaning
of the Tale. There is much more to the Old Man than a conventional personification of Death. It is possible to connect the
Old Man with the allegorical figure of Elde (Old Age),[9] an
archetypal representation of the human predicament where man
is certain of death but totally uncertain of the moment of the
encounter. Elde is closely associated with death, as is the Old
Man, and also, like him, he possesses powerful yet mysterious
insights into the nature of death, such as those imparted to the
revellers:

> 'Now, sires,' quod he, 'if that yow be so leef
> To fynde Deeth, turne up this croked wey,
> For in that grove I lafte hym, by my fey,
> Under a tree, and there he wole abyde;

> Noght for youre boost he wole him no thyng hyde.
> Se ye that ook? Right there ye shal hym fynde.'
>
> (760–5)

At the same time, he cannot be Death himself. Closely linked with the idea of Elde is the figure of the Wandering Jew, with whom the Old Man may be associated since both, though close to death, cannot actually find it.

Chaucer's portrait of the Old Man is deliberately full of suggestion. An air of dark mystery surrounds him, and although the source of this feeling is not made specific, Chaucer clearly invites us to associate him with a variety of figures and meanings. Indeed, this lack of explanation makes the Old Man a most powerful force in the Tale. Yet at the same time he is a real person. Chaucer's description and, more important, the dialogue present to us a picture of an old man tired of life, wishing to die since no young man will exchange his youth for old age. He is rightly indignant at the disrespect of the young men, and then, as though he is frightened of their coarse inhumanity, he is anxious to be on his way. While he speaks to them, we are aware of a striking visualization, a concrete reality, in the dramatic interjections and in the idea of exchanging his clothes for a shroud:

> 'And seye "Leeve mooder, leet me in!
> Lo how I vanysshe, flessh, and blood, and skyn!
> Allas! whan shul my bones been at reste?
> Mooder, with yow wolde I chaunge my cheste
> That in my chambre longe tyme hath be,
> Ye, for an heyre clowt to wrappe in me!"
> But yet to me she wol nat do that grace,
> For which ful pale and welked is my face.'
>
> (731–8)

This passage is unified by the image of Mother Earth, on whose surface the Old Man knocks with his stick, begging for entrance. It is here that we begin to feel a strong sense that the Old Man is not all that he seems. The revellers share this, and they are led to accuse him of being Death's spy. Thus from the initial apparent insignificance of the Old Man we become aware of an increasing air of mystery. We begin to ask questions about the the Old Man, not only who he is, but where he has come from

and where he is going. This response is exactly what Chaucer's design in the Tale demands, and it is for this reason that he refuses to give any specific explanations as to the Old Man's identity. The questions are never answered. As the young revellers rush off to find Death beneath the oak tree, the Old Man walks out of the Tale as mysteriously as he entered it. We are told that he has a destination, but what it is Chaucer does not say. He simply disappears, and as the narrative pace of the verse increases, he is forgotten. His significance has, of course, been completely lost on the revellers, and the irony of the Old Man's final prayer falls on closed hearts.

The brief, speedy narrative of the discovery of the treasure by the three revellers is a marked contrast to the preceding dialogue. In the space of a mere eight lines the whole situation and movement of the Tale is completely changed, and the significance of this new development Chaucer has compressed into a single line: 'No lenger thanne after Deeth they soughte' (772). But its true significance is not immediately apparent. It is only during the ensuing dialogue that we recognize a powerful irony in this statement. The opening words of the worst of the revellers are doubly ironic:

> 'This tresor hath Fortune unto us yiven,
> In myrthe and jolitee oure lyf to lyven,
> And lightly as it comth, so wol we spende.'
>
> (779–81)

The murderous conspiracy which he is already plotting provides a forceful contrast to this deceptive platitude. A few lines later he half betrays his true intentions with a thoughtless slip of the tongue which he hastily conceals in an ironic parenthesis:

> 'But myghte this gold be caried fro this place
> Hoom to myn hous, or elles unto youres—
> For wel ye woot that al this gold is oures—
> Thanne were we in heigh felicitee.'
>
> (784–7)

The broken, halting rhythm here exactly conveys the scheming thoughts of the villain. The rhythm becomes still slower in the next few lines, where the long, sombre vowel sounds create a sense of sinister evil:

'Men wolde seyn that we were theves stronge
And for oure owene tresor doon us honge.'
(789-90)

Then, as he outlines his plan, we sense a quickening of the pulse, and a feeling of excitement is conveyed in the repetition of the word 'cut' and the blunt, matter-of-fact language of the verse.

Again a brief, rapid narrative sequence intervenes before the conspiracy is continued in the dialogue. The development which follows is a masterpiece of subtle suggestion and ironic double-talk. The irony lies primarily in the fact that the first villain begins to play on the mind of the second by appealing to the very qualities of brotherhood and loyalty which bind all three together. We notice how the repetition of the pronoun 'thou' serves to exclude the youngest reveller from the oath sworn in the tavern, and to strengthen the ties between the other two:

'Thow knowest wel thou art my sworen brother;
Thy profit wol I telle thee anon.
Thou woost wel that oure felawe is agon.'
(808-10)

The brief, simple questions of the second reveller reveal not only a misunderstanding of his companion's purpose but also a certain wariness. He obviously senses that something is wrong, but he is not prepared to take the initiative. This has the effect of increasing the suspense, and the tension mounts as it becomes necessary for the instigator of the plot to reveal exactly what he intends. And so Chaucer leads him to a breathless account of his plans, in which the excitement of the conspiracy comes through the verse in the fast-moving syntax and the repetition of the conjunction 'and'. No sooner have they pledged themselves to murder the youngest reveller than Chaucer deftly accomplishes a change of focus. The effect of the conspiracy has been to throw our sympathy onto the victim of the plot, but this is short-lived. In a striking image of the golden coins actually rolling about in the young reveller's imagination, Chaucer shows that he too is pre-occupied with the prospect of wealth, and we find that he is just like his companions.

The narrative of his purchase of the poison and his conversation with the apothecary offers a particularly good example of Chaucer's imagination at work. The apothecary may ask why

the young reveller needs the poison, and thus Chaucer creates the excellent idea of the rats and the polecat. The details bring this whole sequence dramatically alive. We take special note of the apothecary's knowledgeable account of the swift effect of the poison, and the brief description of the three large bottles into which the poison is poured. Careful selection of detail creates realism and also a simplicity of style which contributes a great deal to the terrifying sense of inevitability which invests the tale as it approaches its climax.

The final outcome of the Tale is narrated in a deliberately flat style:

> What nedeth it to sermone of it moore?
> For right as they hadde cast his deeth bifoore,
> Right so they han hym slayn, and that anon.
> And whan that this was doon, thus spak that oon:
> 'Now lat us sitte and drynke, and make us merie,
> And afterward we wol his body berie.'
> And with that word it happed hym, par cas,
> To take the botel ther the poyson was,
> And drank, and yaf his felawe drynke also,
> For which anon they storven bothe two.
>   (879–88)

Here the pace of the narrative becomes even quicker, and it is as though we are watching the revellers rush grotesquely into the arms of Death. And so the Tale moves at great speed to its conclusion, and ironically it is the very end which the villains set out to find on their quest.

At this point in the Tale the speed of the verse slackens, and the style changes back again to the deliberate measured rhythms of the sermon and the conventional techniques of rhetorical expression. The Pardoner's attention focuses once more on his audience. He makes a learned reference to a medical authority, and then addresses his listeners in high rhetorical style with the device of *exclamatio*:

> O cursed synne of alle cursednesse!
> O traytours homycide, O wikkednesse!
> O glotonye, luxurie, and hasardrye!
> Thou blasphemour of Crist with vileynye
> And othes grete, of usage and of pride!
> Allas! mankynde, how may it bitide

> That to thy creatour, which that the wroghte,
> And with his precious herte-blood thee boghte,
> Thou art so fals and so unkynde, allas?
>   (895–903)

Although it is true that the purpose of this device is to enlist a certain emotional response from the audience, the Pardoner's use of it is more complex. For through this passage he effects a difficult transition, from the vivid details and open horror of the Tale back to the more formal rhetorical tone of exhortation in the sermon. The transition is completed when the Pardoner calls on his audience to come forward and receive his pardons. This is a skilful move, for he clearly intends to make use of the emotional response to his Tale:

> Into the blisse of hevene shul ye gon.
> I yow assoille, by myn heigh power,
> Yow that wol offre, as clene and eek as cleer
> As ye were born.
>   (912–15)

But the absolution which the Pardoner offers here is, he claims, full absolution not only from the punishment for a sin (*a poena*) but also from the sin itself (*a culpa*). And this he has no power to give if, as we assume, he is not a priest.

For a moment the truth of his deception dawns upon him:

> And Jhesu Crist, that is oure soules leche,
> So graunte yow his pardoun to receyve,
> For that is best; I wol yow nat deceyve.
>   (916–18)

By ending his Tale with a benediction of this kind, the Pardoner is following a medieval convention.[10] Yet it is impossible to dismiss these three lines as mere convention. They represent a grave and sincere expression of emotion. The Pardoner is human, and for a moment we become aware of this. The change adds to the mystery of the Pardoner, for he is full of contradictions. 'And lo, sires, thus I preche' marks the end of his Tale. What follows suggests some little good in the villain's heart, and the words are strangely moving. His violent cynicism gives way, for a moment, to sincerity.

Here he intends to stop. The very words say so, and so does the rhythm, since what follows is clearly an afterthought: 'But,

sires, o word forgat I in my tale' (919). Now the tone is markedly different, and we have returned to the comedy of the Pardoner's earlier style. Beguiled by the success of his performance, he is completely carried away, and in an orgy of humour and materialism he turns his back on the momentary sincerity. The verse becomes faster as he warms to his subject again. His vanity is forced upon us by his repeated claims that his presence offers a unique security to his fellow pilgrims, any of whom may fall from his horse at any moment and break his neck—an idea which he relishes! Before this sequence reaches its conclusion, however, Chaucer has a further surprise. Just as it appears that all will end in a light comic vein, with the Pardoner reaping a reward which, in view of his masterly entertainment, we may feel is not wholly undeserved, he turns to Harry Bailly. Admittedly this is a foolish move, in view of the antagonism existing between the two pilgrims, but the outcome is an astonishing outburst of violent, vituperative and unrestrained obscenity on the part of the Host. His anger and his attack on the Pardoner is unlike anything he says to anyone else. He has lost his temper, and the blunt coarseness of his comments on the other's physical appearance severely wounds the Pardoner's sensitivity, so that he is stunned to silence. Only the social status of the Knight can reconcile them.

The final irony of the Tale lies in the Pardoner's invitation to Harry Bailly to come forward and be absolved. For although the Pardoner clearly shows with what skill he can manipulate the thoughts and emotions of his congregation, his power is limited. Harry Bailly is not deceived by him, and this the Pardoner fails to recognize. He has deceived himself into a belief that no one can resist his preaching. This is but one small aspect of the total self-deception which we find in the Pardoner. Although we come to recognize this self-deception in the sermon, we cannot fully comprehend its causes, for the Pardoner remains a figure of paradox and, above all, of irony. The irony does not only lie in the fact that he is successful in moving sinners to repentance. There is irony in his own predicament, for just as the three revellers fail to understand that the wages of sin is death, so the Pardoner never sees that he is condemned according to his own terms. It is true that he fully recognizes his own hypocrisy. He is guilty of the sin of avarice, and that, according to his text, is

the root of all evils. What he fails to realize is the full significance of those evils and the damnation which they imply and which is the inevitable consequence of them. He can describe in vivid and dramatic terms the process of sin and its results, and he takes us in his Tale to the very brink of damnation. But he fails to see any connection between this process and his own situation; he is blind to the fact that the quest of the Tale is his own quest.

The complex irony of 'The Pardoner's Tale' adds an important and striking dimension to the other features of narrative and descriptive technique. Yet these qualities together do not account for the total effect of the Tale. We are aware, throughout the Tale, of an insistent atmosphere of mystery and an eerie sense of evil. At certain stages in the tale this is particularly strong. We feel it when the revellers discuss the enemy Death and vow to kill him, and it is there most strongly of all in the meeting with the Old Man. We must associate this sinister sense of mystery and evil with the medieval obsession with death. The effect of 'The Pardoner's Tale' is to intensify this fear. As such, his purpose is in an important way opposed to the approach of the church which he professes to represent. The church's approach was essentially that of the writer of the medieval play *Everyman*, who begins his play with the words: 'Here begynneth a treatyse how ye hye fader of heven sendeth dethe to somon every creature to come and gyve a counte of theyr lyves in this worlde'. Here death is seen as an angel opening the gates of heaven to the faithful and calling all men to justify themselves. Death becomes a messenger of God, something very different from the diabolic force represented in the vision of the Dance of Death and in 'The Pardoner's Tale'. Thus, although the church emphasized the idea that disease and famine were sent by God to punish sinful men, it was concerned at the same time to stress a more positive vision.

Chaucer's approach to the problem of evil and death is in marked contrast to that which we find in *Everyman*. His Tale explores the terrifying inevitability of death and also conveys the sense of mystery and fascination which surround it. Fascination and horror combine in his attitude, just as they combine in so much medieval art, especially in paintings like Bosch's 'Garden of Delights' and Grünewald's 'Temptations of Saint Anthony'.[11] Yet this is not the final note of 'The Pardoner's

Tale'. As we have seen, at the very brink of damnation Chaucer draws back, and retreats rapidly until we are once again watching the human comedy of the pilgrims. At one point the shadow of the Tale seems to darken the scene again as Harry Bailly loses his temper with such unexpected violence. But the former bleak and sinister tone has gone, and it needs only a word from the Knight to set all in harmony once more:

> 'Namoore of this, for it is right ynough!
> Sire Pardoner, be glad and myrie of cheere;
> And ye, sire Hoost, that been to me so deere,
> I prey yow that ye kisse the Pardoner.
> And Pardoner, I prey thee, drawe thee neer,
> And, as we diden, lat us laughe and pleye.'
> Anon they kiste, and ryden forth hir weye.
>
> (962–8)

The Nun's Priest's Tale

Many men sayn that in sweveninges
Ther nys but fables and lesynges;
But men may some swevenes sen
Whiche hardely that false ne ben,
But afterward ben apparaunt. . . .
For this trowe I, and say for me,
That dremes signifiaunce be
Of good and harm to many wightes,
That dremen in her slep a-nyghtes
Ful many thynges covertly,
That fallen after al openly.

> (The *Romaunt of the Rose*,
> Chaucer's translation:
> Fragment A,
> lines 1–5 and 15–20.)

After the Monk's tedious series of unconnected tragic stories has been interrupted by the Knight, Harry Bailly calls on the Nun's Priest to entertain the company of pilgrims with a merry Tale:

> 'Com neer, thou preest, com hyder, thou sir John!
> Telle us swich thyng as may oure hertes glade.'
>
> (2810–11)

Good Sir John accepts the Host's request and proceeds immediately to his story, the fable of the Cock and the Fox.

The fable is not original, and much discussion surrounds the question of Chaucer's source for his Tale. Two fables which closely resemble Chaucer's may be found in the collection of Aesop's stories translated by William Caxton in 1484. In addition scholars have suggested continental literary sources from which Chaucer could have drawn his basic material. Of these, the most important are the French *Le Roman de Renard*, written in the last quarter of the twelfth century, and the thirteenth-century German *Reinhardt Fuchs*.[1]

The many problems surrounding the investigation of Chaucer's sources in 'The Nun's Priest's Tale' need not concern us in detail. What is important is the originality of Chaucer's approach to his material. Although Chaucer's narrative takes the basic form of a conventional beast fable, he refuses to be bound by the formal restrictions of the genre. His animals, for example, take on personalities of their own, and this is something quite new. Even *The Owl and the Nightingale*, one of the most delightful of the longer medieval beast fables, lacks the human quality of Chaucer's fable. It is true that the bickering of the owl and the nightingale comes very close to real human behaviour; the nightingale may remind us of a human being when she indulges in petty abuse:

> 'Vn-wiȝt,' ho sede, 'a-wei þu flo!
> Me is þe wrs þat ich þe so.
> Iwis for þine wle lete
> Wel oft ich mine song forlete;

Min horte atfliþ an falt mi tonge,
Wonne þu art to me iþrunge.'[2]

But the two participants in the debate never cease to be birds.
We most frequently find the attribution of human qualities to
animals in the short illustrative stories in medieval sermons, the
exempla. These are discussed in more detail later in this chapter,
but here it is appropriate to note G. R. Owst's explanation of the
nature of the particular device of combining the animal and the
human in these stories:

> Many of these fables, simple enough in their construction, present
> us with the natural humour and vivid imagination of those who watch
> animal and insect world with the eyes of lively, mischievous children.
> The animals themselves are regarded as little people, precisely as
> they appear in frequent representations upon the margins of illu-
> minated manuscripts, engrossed in earnest conversation, fighting in
> miniature tourneys, playing on musical instruments, indulging in the
> various pastimes and mischiefs of men and women of the day.[3]

The technique which Owst describes here is well illustrated in
the following short extract from a sermon:

> Bartholomeus, *de Proprietatibus Rerum*, seys that ever betwix the
> eddure and the Elephaunte, be keende, is grett strive. The neddur
> is fowle and maliciouse, and the Elephaunte is stronge, fayre, and
> no-thinge grevous. The neddyr, as this clerke seyth, will com and
> make hym for to pleye with the elephaunte, and anon he pleys with
> the neddure; ffor he thenketh non ewill. But at the last this malicious
> worme, the neddyr, styngeth the elephaunte in the eye, as thei pley
> to-gethur, with is tayll. And so sodenly the eddur distrowith the
> elephaunte.[4]

Owst gives many examples of this kind of beast fable, and clearly
the device was commonplace in the Middle Ages. Chaucer, then,
is taking over an established technique, and using it within his
own design. His originality lies in the fusion of the two elements
which, though placed together in beast fables, always remain
distinct.

No less original is Chaucer's narrative technique. His poem is
one of great variety and contrast. Different scenes and subjects
are juxtaposed with startling effect, so that we find ourselves
thrown from realistic description in a farmyard to colourful
courtly scenes, from humble colloquial dialogue to high rhetoric,

from scholarly learning to practical country lore, and from biblical references to classical legends. Yet this diversity of subject matter is controlled throughout the Tale, and Chaucer ensures an overall unity of design by means of his constantly changing approach to his material, the changing focus of the narrative technique.

At the beginning of the Tale Chaucer sets the scene and introduces the characters. We are immediately faced with the first of the poem's many contrasts, that between the widow and her cottage, and Chauntecleer and his 'court'. Chaucer seems at first to be offering a simple, factual description of the widow:

> A povre wydwe, somdeel stape in age
> Was whilom dwellyng in a narwe cotage,
> Biside a grove, stondynge in a dale.
> (2821–3)

It is not vague and general, but full of fascinating details:

> Thre large sowes hadde she, and namo,
> Three keen, and eek a sheep that highte Malle.
> (2830–1)

He chooses simple but highly descriptive words like 'stape' and 'narwe', and we notice in particular the harsh consonant sounds of 'stape' and 'sklendre', which recreate the poverty and hardship endured by the widow. But although poor, Chaucer's widow is contented:

> Attempree diete was al hir phisik,
> And exercise, and hertes suffisaunce.
> (2838–9)

The widow lives simply within her means, and it is to this temperance that Chaucer attributes her sound health and moral strength. She is therefore associated with the homely plainness of a group of characters in the *Canterbury Tales*, which includes the Parson, of whom we are told in the Prologue: 'He koude in litel thyng have suffisaunce' (490). The idea of temperance, or 'mesure', which they represent, was a fundamental moral positive in the Middle Ages. Some critics have suggested that Chaucer is offering the widow's approach to life as an ideal,[5] but the very real sense of *enforced* frugality does not seem to support this. We are clearly invited to admire the widow, but

Chaucer is too much a realist to leave the matter here. There
is a qualification in his attitude to the widow's situation. He does
not explicitly show this, but it is contained implicitly within the
poetic style, for much of Chaucer's description of the widow is
in the negative:

> N'apoplexie shente nat hir heed.
> No wyn ne drank she, neither whit ne reed . . .
>
> (2841–2)

The use of negatives (the rhetorical device of *oppositio*) makes us
increasingly aware of the drudgery and harshness of her life.
There is, then, much more to the description of the widow than
the apparent simplicity of the opening lines suggests.

Still more complex is the ensuing description of Chauntecleer.
Chaucer divides this into three sections. The first deals with
Chauntecleer's crowing, and since it is his voice which eventually causes the catastrophe it is highly appropriate that we should
associate this quality with him from the outset. It is equally
appropriate that the Nun's Priest should compare Chauntecleer's
voice with features of religious life like a church organ and an
abbey clock. The second of these comparisons prompts Chaucer
to include a glimpse of Chauntecleer's astronomical skill:

> By nature he knew ech ascencioun
> Of the equynoxial in thilke toun . . .
>
> (2855–6)

This detail also looks forward to the Tale where Chauntecleer
shows himself to be a wise and knowledgeable bird well-versed
in many aspects of medieval lore. The second part of the description is concerned with physical appearance and colour. Chauntecleer's comb is compared to the castellations of a fortress. The
colours are bright and sharp, like those of so many medieval
manuscript illuminations, and their brightness is made more
emphatic by Chaucer's use of comparatives: the red of his comb
is 'redder than the fyn coral' and his nails are 'whitter than the
lylye flour'. There are no colours at all in the description of the
widow. On the contrary, her dwelling is dull and dingy: 'Ful
sooty was hire bour and eek hir halle' (2832). What is more, the
association of Chauntecleer with impressive medieval architecture (a church and a castle) offers a striking contrast to the

widow's narrow cottage. Finally, Chaucer turns to Chauntecleer's companions, Pertelote and the six hens. He now uses
French courtly words like 'plesaunce', 'debonaire' and 'compaignable'; Chauntecleer becomes the lover, Pertelote his lady,
and so Chaucer brings into the description the whole medieval
tradition of Courtly Love. He chooses two adjectives which are
central to this tradition. 'Gentil', here applied to Chauntecleer,
suggests the idea of noble behaviour befitting a person of high
rank. Pertelote is described as 'curteys', an epithet similar in
meaning to 'gentil'. 'Curteys' refers more specifically to behaviour at court, and implies, particularly, knowledge of *Amour
Courtois*, the medieval game of love. Thus 'curteys' is doubly
appropriate, since it contributes to the creation of the heroic
tone, and at the same time amplifies the specifically sexual
theme which comes to the fore in this passage in words like
'plesaunce' and 'paramours'.

When we compare these two descriptive paragraphs, and we
are clearly intended to do so, we become increasingly aware of a
dual focus or changing perspective in the way we look at the
characters. Structurally, the two sections are very similar, for
Chaucer devotes the first three lines to an introduction of each
subject, and he then proceeds to a more detailed description.
But in subject matter they are in marked contrast. To describe
the widow and her situation first is a necessary part of Chaucer's
design, since it is only in contrast to her poverty that we appreciate the rich splendour of Chauntecleer. It is this splendour
which elevates Chauntecleer's position, and makes him a prince
in his own court, with Pertelote as his lady. But at the same time,
the realistic description of the widow has presented the farmyard
as it really is. Chauntecleer and Pertelote are chickens, and their
court is a humble yard. This is not, however, the total effect of
Chaucer's irony. We are faced, in these two verse paragraphs,
with a real world and a dream world, and the boundaries between
the two are uncertain. The description of Chauntecleer, for
example, seems highly improbable, yet it has been pointed out
that the colours accord exactly with a particular English breed
of chicken, the Golden Spangled Hamburg. When this is recognized we are bound to look at Chauntecleer in yet another light.
And there is an ironical change of focus in the initial presentation
of the widow. Here Chaucer uses the words 'bour' and 'halle'

to describe the cottage, words which are more usually associated
with castles and courts. This dual focus is clearly a major part
of Chaucer's design. For although we remain aware of the true
reality behind the poem, we have no difficulty in accepting the
heroic portrait of Chauntecleer and Pertelote. The world of the
poem is one in which we can accept anything, a fairy-tale world of
singing and sunshine:

> For thilke tyme, as I have understonde,
> Beestes and briddes koude speke and synge.
>   (2880–1)

With his introduction thus complete, and our familiarity with
the characters and setting firmly established, we sense a quickening of the pulse within the verse. Towards the end of the second
verse paragraph, Chaucer has produced a slower rhythm, an
effect achieved first by the use of the long French words like
'governaunce' and 'compaignable', and then by the halting consonants in the confidential final line (2881). It is in contrast to
this that we appreciate the new movement of the verse as the
narrative itself gathers momentum. Chaucer wastes no time
in elaboration, but takes us straight to the dramatic incident
which forms the starting point of the whole Tale, Chauntecleer's
dream. In the long vowel sounds of 'soore' and 'roore', together
with the grating consonants of 'gan gronen in his throte',
Chaucer actually recreates the sound of Chauntecleer's groans,
and thus we find ourselves dramatically caught up in the sequence of events. Our interest is further engaged by the homely
dialogue which follows, where we witness the conversation not
of a cock and hen, but of a husband and wife. Chauntecleer is
still the prince of the courtly convention; his style of address to
Pertelote is very formal and courteous:

> And he answerde, and seyde thus: 'Madame,
> I pray yow that ye take it nat agrief.'
>   (2892–3)

But in her practical concern for her husband's ailment we see
Pertelote more clearly as a simple housewife. The breathless
excitement of Chauntecleer's account of his dream is skilfully
conveyed through the verse with its fast rhythm and sequence
of enjambement. Chauntecleer gives an accurate description of

the creature he has seen, and we find again in the Tale a strong
interest in colours:

> 'His colour was bitwixe yelow and reed,
> And tipped was his tayl and bothe his eeris
> With blak, unlyk the remenant of his heeris . . .'
>
> (2902–4)

Particularly prominent in Chauntecleer's memory are the black
tips of the tail and ears, a feature emphasized by the enjambement
which throws rhythmic stress onto the word 'blak'. Pertelote replies with a series of lively interjections: 'Avoy', 'fy on yow', 'Allas',
and 'by that God above'. In this way she establishes her tone of
affectionate derision towards her cowardly husband. The significance of these lines is, however, increased when we remember
the thread of the Courtly Love tradition which runs through the
Tale. Pertelote proceeds from her original attack on Chauntecleer's cowardice to enumerate a number of qualities which, she
claims, are those which all women desire of their husbands:

> 'We alle desiren, if it myghte bee,
> To han housbondes hardy, wise, and free,
> And secree, and no nygard, ne no fool . . .'
>
> (2913–15)

'Free' implies generosity, and is one of the attributes of a man of
'gentilesse'. The quality of discretion ('secree'), too, played a
major role in the medieval game of *Amour Courtois*. Chaucer
gives us a full description of the ideal man according to courtly
tradition in *Troilus and Criseyde*, and it is interesting to compare
Pertelote's statement with, for example, the views implicit in
Criseyde's reaction on seeing Troilus for the first time after she
has been told by Pandarus that Troilus loves her:

> But swich a knyghtly sighte, trewely . . .
> So lik a man of armes and a knyght
> He was to seen, fulfilled of heigh prowesse;
> For bothe he hadde a body and a myght
> To don that thyng, as wel as hardynesse;
> And ek to seen hym in his gere hym dresse,
> So fressh, so yong, so weldy semed he,
> It was an heven upon hym for to see.
>
> (*Tr*, Book 2,
> 628, 631–7)

Chaucer's audience would be very familiar with these ideas. Consequently, they would easily associate them with Pertelote's statement in lines 2908–21. And so all the courtly overtones of the quality of courage itself come to the fore in this passage.

What is the attitude to love and women which Chaucer is presenting in 'The Nun's Priest's Tale'? Some scholars have suggested that the Tale forms part of the Marriage Group, the sequence of Tales which together presents a lengthy debate on marriage.[6] But Chaucer is not primarily concerned with this subject in his fable of the Cock and the Fox. Although at the beginning of the Tale Chauntecleer has seven 'sustres' and 'paramours', six of them soon fade into the distance, and Chaucer concerns himself with one of these companions, Pertelote. Similarly the Tale begins with the prince and lady of courtly tradition, but the relationship soon becomes a more homely and realistic one of husband and wife, as Pertelote advises Chauntecleer to take laxatives for his health. In the simple rhythms of the dialogue, too, the picture of husband and wife is further emphasized, although the courtly element is never lost, and Chauntecleer continues to address his wife with great courtesy when he disagrees with her interpretation of his dream: ' "Madame," quod he, "graunt mercy of youre loore" ' (2970).

When Chauntecleer has concluded his series of examples in the Dream Debate, he returns to the subject of love and the qualities of his wife:

> 'Madame Pertelote, so have I blis,
> Of o thyng God hath sent me large grace;
> For whan I se the beautee of youre face,
> Ye been so scarlet reed aboute youre yen,
> It maketh al my drede for to dyen;
> For al so siker as *In principio*,
> *Mulier est hominis confusio*,—
> Madame, the sentence of this Latyn is,
> "Womman is mannes joye and al his blis." '
>   (3158–66)

He is fascinated by the physical beauty of Pertelote, whom we see much more as a woman than a hen in this passage. His emotional response to his wife captivates him, and he is ruled by this passion. This is not to say that Pertelote has sovereignty over her husband (a subject discussed by Chaucer at length in 'The

Wife of Bath's Tale' and 'The Franklin's Tale'). But reason in Chauntecleer is secondary to emotion. The same, Chaucer implies, was true of the relationship between Adam and Eve. We are justified in recalling the Eden story here since the Latin quotation plainly invites us to do so: 'In principio' is the opening phrase of the Book of Genesis. Now, in the second creation story, Eve was indeed Adam's 'joye and al his blis'. But she was also the cause of Adam's fall, and this is what the Latin text really means. There is a double irony in this mistranslation of the Latin. First, for all his wide knowledge which he has fully displayed to us, Chauntecleer misinterprets the warning implicit in the text, just as he fails to heed the warning of impending disaster in his dream. And, secondly, it is the physical attractiveness of his wife which distracts his attention from the dream, and causes him to forget the portent. What is more, there is a further irony in Chauntecleer's attempt to win back Pertelote's favour, after the argument about dreams, by flattering her. This, of course, is precisely the means whereby the Fox beguiles Chauntecleer:

> This Chauntecleer his wynges gan to bete,
> As man that koude his traysoun nat espie,
> So was he ravysshed with his flaterie.
>
> (3322–4)

As Chauntecleer continues to talk about the physical side of his relationship with Pertelote, we are reminded, on the human level, of the poor widow with whom the story began. Chaucer recognizes with rich compassion the poverty and hardship of the condition endured not only by her, but by so many of his less fortunate contemporaries. Just as there is scarcely room for physical contact on the birds' perch, so there is little opportunity for pleasure amid the struggle for existence experienced by thousands in the Middle Ages. So important is this connection that Chaucer uses the same word, 'narwe', for the perch and for the widow's cottage. The whole situation makes a mockery of the initial exaggerated heroic description and of Chauntecleer's idea of himself as a prince in his court. The narrow perch and the widow's cottage are the realities of the Tale.

Yet even as he deflates the situation from one point of view, Chaucer is building it up from another angle. There is, of course, the biblical quotation and the subtly implied parallel between

Chauntecleer and Pertelote and Adam and Eve, a comparison
which plays an important part in the creation of the mock-heroic
tone of the Tale. But Chaucer goes further than this. As soon as
Chauntecleer flies from his perch and is surrounded by his
paramours he is once again the courtly prince. The idea of a
king is insistently created: '*Real* he was, he was namoore aferd'
and 'Thus *roial*, as a *prince* is in his *halle*' (3176, 3184). And as
he struts up and down, Chauntecleer is compared to a fierce lion.
This exaggerated description invites us to recall all that has gone
before, and we see still more clearly the inflated nature of the
whole fantasy. Even as this happens, however, Chaucer is skilfully forestalling us. He is fully aware of the dramatic effect of
these swift changes of focus, and thus he places at the centre
of the verse paragraph, in simple, blunt terms ('fethered' and
'trad') the physical reality of two chickens mating in the dust of
the farmyard:

> He fethered Pertelote twenty tyme,
> And trad hire eke as ofte, er it was pryme . . .
>
> (3177–8)

Within the changing perspectives of the narrative we are aware
of two distinct attitudes to women. As we have seen, Chauntecleer's statement that 'Womman is mannes joye and al his blis'
(3166) is ironic. This is not, however, the final word about
women in the Tale. At a later stage Chaucer offers a deliberately
striking contrast:

> My tale is of a cok, as ye may heere,
> That tok his conseil of his wyf, with sorwe,
> To walken in the yerd upon that morwe
> That he hadde met that dreem that I yow tolde.
> Wommennes conseils been ful ofte colde;
> Wommannes conseil broghte us first to wo,
> And made Adam fro Paradys to go,
> Ther as he was ful myrie and wel at ese.
>
> (3252–9)

Here the narrator explicitly attributes to the advice of women all
human problems and the original fall of man from grace. Original
Sin and Adam's loss of Paradise are references which continue
the heroic tone of the poem, while on another level this passage
must be read as a commentary on everyday problems inherent in

the relationship between men and women. In both readings, the narrator lays the blame squarely on the female sex. This is the view of the Nun's Priest, who throughout the Tale reveals a marked dislike of women. There is, for example, his attitude to the book of Launcelot de Lake, 'That wommen holde in ful greet reverence' (3213). The priest considers the book to be especially suitable for women, who enjoy the entertainment of fanciful romantic tales. This is not, however, Chaucer's view, and when we recognize this, we see a possible solution to the strange statement: 'I kan noon harm of no womman divyne' (3266). Although this comment appears to be the Nun's Priest's, it is quite out of character. We must therefore be aware of a third personality present in the narrative of the Tale, that of Chaucer himself. For this stark, simple statement must represent Chaucer's own view, as opposed to that of the persona he has adopted in this Tale. Chaucer is here discussing one of the major themes of medieval thought and literature, the problem of women and their position (a subject explored at greater length in the Wife of Bath's Prologue). The patristic tradition of St Jerome is that represented in this Tale by the Nun's Priest, which looks upon women as the source of all evil since Eve consumed the apple. According to this view, the only point of marriage is to beget children who may be virgin or celibate. We find this attitude frequently expressed in the violent anti-feminist preaching of the Middle Ages. G. R. Owst quotes an extract from a sermon of Dr William Lichfield which illustrates this view:

> Eve, oure oldest moder in paradise, held long tale with the eddre, and told hym qwhat god had seyd to hire and to hire husband of etyng the apple; and bi hire talkyng the fend understod hire febylnes and hire unstabilnes, and fond therby a way to bryng hir to confusioun.[7]

In contrast to this, a moderate position is taken up by St Paul, who argued that marriage is a justifiable accommodation for the weakness of fallen man. Finally, there is the idealization of woman and the formalization of love which we find in the Courtly Love tradition (in, for example, the *Roman de la Rose*). We should remember here, however, that Courtly Love was essentially a literary tradition, and one more common in France than in

England. The reality of English life in the Middle Ages presented a very different picture, with women held as mere chattels (a position reinforced by the patristic tradition of contempt). What is more, there existed side by side with the courtly style primitive eroticism inherited from an earlier age.[8] This is the paradox which Chaucer recalls in the direct juxtaposition of the courtly illusions and physical reality in the farmyard.

We left the Dream Debate at the point where Pertelote condemns Chauntecleer's cowardice. She sums up her attack with an emphatic couplet in which Chaucer exactly captures the derisive incredulity of the wife who is too practical to be convinced by dreams:

> 'Allas! and konne ye been agast of swevenys?
> Nothyng, God woot, but vanitee in sweven is.'
>
> (2921–2)

This strong tri-syllabic rhyme marks the conclusion of one sequence of thought, and now Pertelote turns from her scolding to a more sympathetic diagnosis of the cause of Chauntecleer's dream. The rhythm of the verse takes on a slower pace, and the long words like 'replecciouns', 'complecciouns' and 'super-fluytee' convey a sense of confidence in the practical value of her knowledge. Although Pertelote's analysis of the situation is eventually proved wrong, her interpretation accords in every detail with contemporary theories of medical science. Pertelote clearly knows, for example, the basic medieval belief that the human body was composed of a mixture of four humours, blood, phlegm, choler and black bile or melancholy. Physical health was dependent on the maintenance of a steady balance of the four humours in the individual physiological composition of a human being. Mental health was directly connected with this, and thus it is that Pertelote associates the mental phenomenon of the dream with an imbalance or 'superfluytee' in the body's physiological composition. Colours are again important here, for the red and black colours of the animal in Chauntecleer's dream indicate to Pertelote certain significant associations. The red colour she attributes to an excess of choler, the red humour, and then she connects the black element with the melancholic humour, black bile.[9]

As we watch this fascinating display of medieval scientific lore,

we never lose sight of the character in the drama to whom we are listening. Here, as elsewhere, Pertelote has all the qualities of the practical housewife concerned for her husband's health. She is carried away with her examples:

> 'For feere of blake beres, or boles blake,
> Or elles blake develes wole hem take.'
>
> (2935–6)

Here the alliteration emphasizes her enthusiasm. And there is a very human touch in the couplet:

> 'Of othere humours koude I telle also
> That werken many a man sleep ful wo . . .'
>
> (2937–8)

Pertelote indicates the extent of her knowledge in order to lend weight to her argument and thus convince Chauntecleer, and yet at the same time she is anxious to proceed to her main point, the remedy. So she advises Chauntecleer to take a laxative, which will correct the excess of humours from which he is suffering:

> 'I conseille yow the beste, I wol nat lye,
> That bothe of colere and of malencolye
> Ye purge yow . . .'
>
> (2945–7)

Pertelote further reveals her practical knowledge when she offers to provide the healing herbs herself, and in conclusion she consolidates her authority by giving a list of fascinating details of herbal lore:

> 'A day or two ye shul have digestyves
> Of wormes, er ye take youre laxatyves
> Of lawriol, centaure, and fumetere,
> Or elles of ellebor, that groweth there,
> Of katapuce, or of gaitrys beryis,
> Of herbe yve, growyng in oure yeerd, ther mery is;
> Pekke hem up right as they growe and ete hem yn.'
>
> (2961–7)

Here the verse accelerates, the punctuation gives a sense of breathless excitement, and in the last two lines the rhythmic pattern of the verse itself is stretched as the agitation reaches its climax.

Chauntecleer now takes up the argument, and begins one of the longest digressions in the Tale. His approach to the Dream Debate contrasts dramatically with that of his wife. She possesses, as we have seen, all the practical knowledge, but Chauntecleer's learning is imaginative. It has been collected from books. In the light of this, it is appropriate that the two extended examples which he gives at the heart of his argument should be narrative episodes from literary sources. These episodes display Chaucer's narrative technique at its best. In both there is a skilful use of dialogue, which gives dramatic life to the stories and an added dimension to the characters. In the first episode the dialogue is straightforward and, as with the speech of Chauntecleer and Pertelote, Chaucer follows the rhythms and idiom of simple speech:

> ' "Allas! for in an oxes stalle
> This nyght I shal be mordred ther I lye.
> Now help me, deere brother, or I dye." '
> (3004–6)

Particularly effective here is the impact of the blunt simplicity of the last line. At the climax of the story, Chaucer heightens the tension and plays upon our expectation with the device of repetition. Three times within eight lines Chaucer mentions the murder for which we are all waiting. Finally, however, the narrative is stripped of all but the bare facts, and, as at the climax of 'The Pardoner's Tale', the inevitable conclusion is bluntly stated, in the space of three stark lines:

> 'The peple out sterte and caste the cart to grounde,
> And in the myddel of the dong they founde
> The dede man, that mordred was al newe.'
> (3047–9)

The same techniques are employed in the second narrative episode. Chaucer captures the urgency of the warning of impending disaster by presenting it in blunt, dramatic speech:

> . . . ' "If thou tomorwe wende,
> Thow shalt be dreynt; my tale is at an ende." '
> (3081–2)

Similarly, in the dialogue of the two merchants Chaucer achieves a compelling immediacy by his use of colloquial idiom ('I sette

nat a straw by thy dremynges' (3090) and by the exactness of human nature recorded in the short dismissal 'and have good day!' At the climax we again notice Chaucer's simple, bald narrative. He offers no comment or explanation, but narrates only the bare facts of the disaster:

> 'But casuelly the shippes botme rente,
> And ship and man under the water wente . . .'
> (3101-2)

These two stories are part of Chauntecleer's argument. We therefore associate the narrative skill of their presentation with Chauntecleer, and in consequence we recognize the vigorous involvement of the character who becomes so fascinated by his skill and by the very sound of his voice that he is completely carried away. As he begins his first story, Chauntecleer follows quite closely the initial subject of the Debate. We see this in his repeated references to chance, luck and fortune. Such phrases as 'in a ful good entente', 'as it wolde falle' and 'As was his aventure or his fortune' focus our attention, like Chauntecleer's, on the future. And, of course, at this stage in the Debate Chauntecleer is particularly concerned with the possibility of impending catastrophe in the farmyard. But by the time he reaches the end of his first tale he is so involved in his narrative that what began as an example of the prophetic truth of dreams has now become an argument against murder: ' "Mordre wol out, this my conclusioun" ' (3057). Chauntecleer has forgotten his original purpose. It is his own skill which commands him now, for he has his audience, and we have been told early in the Tale that his voice has no equal.

Within the structural context of 'The Nun's Priest's Tale' as a whole, Chauntecleer's stories play a key role. The effect is one of intense irony. The Tale of the Cock and the Fox seems to be moving, as the original dream foretold, towards a tragic climax. In the event, as we know, disaster is averted. But the possibility of disaster plays a major part in the Tale. It is in this light that we see the true function of Chauntecleer's stories. They are tales of violence and death, and dramatically they create a sense of impending doom. They make it clear to us that a comparable fate may well await Chauntecleer.

As he reaches the end of his second tale, Chauntecleer seems to

be on the point of concluding his argument. He refers, at last, to
Pertelote, who has receded into the background during the narrative sequence, and then he sums up the purpose of his examples:

'By swiche ensamples olde maistow leere
That no man sholde been to recchelees
Of dremes; for I seye thee, doutelees,
That many a dreem ful soore is for to drede.'

(3106–9)

But Chauntecleer is by no means content to end here. He has
more learning to display, and there are further examples to
make his argument still more convincing. The technique is
similar to that employed in 'The Franklin's Tale', for Chauntecleer now proceeds to give six more examples of the prophetic
value of dreams, examples drawn from a variety of sources.
Here, however, Chaucer's narrative method changes. He is no
longer concerned to give a detailed, dramatic account. By contrast, he presents these new examples with bold simplicity,
emphasizing not the narrative details, but the authoritative nature
of his sources. No one, he argues, can resist the combined authority of Macrobeus, the Old Testament and the Classics. Once
again during the course of these examples Chauntecleer appears
to be reaching his conclusion, but with the commanding excla-
mation 'Lo Cresus' he proceeds to give two more illustrations,
the first of which takes up the subject of the last stanzas of 'The
Monk's Tale' which immediately precedes that of the Nun's
Priest. Chauntecleer's personality directs the course of the narrative in this sequence, for we are constantly aware of his presence.
The excitement of the verse, the eager rhythms, the compelling
dialogue with its bluntness and its colloquial idioms, all help to
keep the proud hero in focus. It is only necessary for Chaucer
to make direct reference to the teller of the tale at infrequent
intervals. One such occasion is when Chauntecleer offers a delightful interjection emphasizing the truth of his second story:
' "I gabbe nat, so have I joye or blis" ' (3066). During the final
succession of shorter examples, there is a more insistent sense of
the presence of Chauntecleer in the use of dramatic exclamations
and imperatives: ' "Looke of Egipte the kyng" ' and ' "Lo heere
Andromacha" ', and by the inclusion of short persuasive comments such as: ' "I sey yow trewely" ', ' "I pray yow" ' and ' "I

sey nat alle" '. And then, true to his character, even at the end
of this *tour de force* Chauntecleer is still reluctant to leave his
subject:

> 'But thilke tale is al to longe to telle,
> And eek it is ny day, I may nat dwelle.'
>
> (3149–50)

Chaucer often uses this device as a means of passing from one
subject to the next, but it is, of course, particularly appropriate
to Chauntecleer.

At this stage, Chauntecleer recalls his own dream and repeats
his feelings of apprehension. But its initial terrifying impact has
faded away, and with the coming of daylight, and the thought
of his wife's beauty, Chauntecleer's fear is finally dispelled.
Ironically, the sound of his own voice and his pride have made
him overconfident. He has failed to heed the warning, and disaster cannot be far away.

What is the point of this long section on dreams? Chaucer and
his contemporaries were fascinated by dreams and their interpretation. Indeed, dreams formed a popular subject in medieval
literature not only in Chaucer's own earlier works like the *Book
of the Duchess* and the *Parliament of Fowls*, but also in poems
like the Gawain-poet's *Pearl* and the French *Le Roman de la
Rose*, which Chaucer knew and loved. At the end of this section,
Chaucer leaves the issue open to question. He provides no answer,
even though the dream proves in this case to be prophetic. In
the Debate we again see the interplay of opposites which forms
such an important part of Chaucer's design in 'The Nun's
Priest's Tale'. Chauntecleer and Pertelote, as characters, occupy
extreme positions. Pertelote is clearly at fault when she attributes
the dream to a single psychological disorder easily rectified by
laxatives. What is more, the outcome of the Tale proves that her
dismissal of the dream is totally and disastrously wrong. But
Chauntecleer is equally ignorant of reality. As he pursues his
argument, he is so carried away by his scholarly stories and
examples that he forgets the original cause of the debate. And
when he sees the Fox among the weeds in the farmyard, he fails
to connect the animal with the vision in his dream. Yet he
described the creature accurately to Pertelote, and therefore he
has no excuse for his failure to face reality. Both the Cock and

his wife live in a self-induced dream world, which Chaucer contrasts from the outset with the widow's approach to life. It is a contrast between reality and fantasy, a theme which frequently engaged Chaucer's imagination in his comic Tales.

The dual focus created by the presence of the human and the animal in Chauntecleer and Pertelote demands a complex response from the listeners to the Tale. We are invited to laugh not at the subject of dreams itself, but at the incongruity of such a debate carried on between two birds. At the same time, there is the very real human characteristic of dogmatism and exclusiveness of attitude, particularly on the part of Chauntecleer. Here is yet one more aspect of the human comedy of the *Canterbury Tales.*

When Chaucer eventually returns to his narrative (line 3187), he continues to build up the heroic tone. He does this by a further reference to Adam and Eve and the Creation story, and by giving another glimpse of Chauntecleer the prince strutting about his court surrounded by his wives. But the heroic effect is most skilfully created by the elaborate designation of the month, day and time on which the impending disaster will occur. The reference to the signs of the Zodiac, and to the sun, involves the whole universe in the fate of Chauntecleer, and this is summed up by the simple universal reference of the couplet:

> For evere the latter ende of joye is wo.
> God woot that worldly joye is soone ago . . .
>
> (3205–6)

Yet the whole passage is, of course, inflated. Chauntecleer's address to Pertelote exactly conveys his self-important pride. In addition we become conscious of Chaucer's own voice in the subtle satirising of medieval astronomy and the complicated method of calculating time. Finally, the absurdity of the whole situation is captured in these lines:

> And if a rethor koude faire endite,
> He in a cronycle saufly myghte it write
> As for a sovereyn notabilitee.
>
> (3207–9)

Chaucer's humour lies in the complete disproportion between the reality of the dusty chickens and the high heroic style in which these activities are described.

The final irony of the Dream Debate comes when Chauntecleer fails to recognize the Fox as the red and black animal of his vision. A new urgency comes upon the verse now. The descriptive details are few but carefully chosen:

> And in a bed of wortes stille he lay,
> Till it was passed undren of the day . . .
>
> (3221-2)

and the narrative appears to be approaching its climax with speed. But Chaucer creates further dramatic suspense by introducing new digressions. We are now entertained with another display of knowledge, although this time the speaker is not Chauntecleer. It is, in fact, not clear whether we are listening to the Nun's Priest or Chaucer himself. What is certain, however, is the tone of this passage, straightforward and presented with a convincing air of authority. It continues and develops the idea of the prophetic value of dreams, and it also takes up the ideas of chance, luck and fortune which we noticed at the beginning of Chauntecleer's first story. The absence of Chauntecleer's personality removes this part of the Tale from immediate association with the humorous situation of the Cock and the Fox, and thus we may view it as a more serious statement on a subject of very real interest to his audience. Chaucer has interrupted his Tale for a brief but scholarly summary of three contemporary views on Predestination and Foreknowledge.

The problem of man's freedom of action in relation to God's omniscience is extremely complex. There are three main positions which thinkers throughout the ages have taken up. All grant that God knows what actions man will perform in the future, but differ in their estimations of how strictly God's foreknowledge compels him to act. Bishop Bradwardine cut the gordian knot by almost denying human freedom: God knows that certain actions will be performed, and this knowledge makes those actions inevitable. Our freedom is therefore illusory. St Augustine considered that freedom itself is part of the human condition and so, though God knows the future, he knows too (because He willed it) that we can choose what we will do. Boethius allowed the greatest scope to human freedom, for God's foreknowledge does not directly determine action, but only conditionally. These ideas play an important part in this Tale.

At last Chaucer promises to take up the Tale again:

> I wol nat han to do of swich mateere;
> My tale is of a cok, as ye may heere . . .
>
> (3251–2)

Yet even now he turns aside, this time for a further glance at the evil influence of women. Finally, we do return to the story; the pace of the verse quickens, and the texture of the poetry changes. Chaucer now eliminates all but the most important descriptive details, with the effect that a few salient facts like the butterfly in the vegetables stand out as the suspense grows. And he reintroduces the dimension of the mock-heroic in the parallel with the Garden of Eden and the innocence of Chauntecleer's failure to recognize the Fox as the creature of his dream. The verse changes again as the Fox begins to address Chauntecleer in flattering tones. The Fox plays upon the ideas of courtly behaviour in his use of words like 'gentil' and 'vileynye', and thus introduces a thread of irony into the passage. This grows stronger as it develops through the speech: ' "So moote I brouke wel myne eyen tweye" ', and ' "Lat se, konne ye youre fader countrefete?" ' (3300, 3321), and it reaches a further intensification in the reference to the story of Burnellus the Donkey. Then, with dramatic simplicity and speed, Chaucer shows that the Fox's words have achieved their design:

> This Chauntecleer his wynges gan to bete,
> As man that koude his traysoun nat espie,
> So was he ravysshed with his flaterie.
>
> (3322–4)

Here we are again aware of the double view of Chauntecleer as a strutting cock and also as a real human being.

All is now prepared for disaster, but Chaucer's narrative skill demands another short interlude to build up the suspense to its highest pitch. Thus he briefly condemns the evils of flattery, proceeding in the manner of a moral exhortation in a medieval sermon:

> Allas! ye lordes, many a fals flatour
> Is in youre courtes, and many a losengeour,
> That plesen yow wel moore, by my feith,
> Than he that soothfastnesse unto yow seith.
> Redeth Ecclesiaste of flaterye . . .
>
> (3325–9)

This is by no means the only occasion in the Tale where Chaucer enhances his effect by drawing on the techniques of the sermon. Neither is his interest in sermons confined to this Tale: 'The Pardoner's Tale', in particular, offers a full exploration of the possibilities of the sermon form. One of the most important devices in medieval sermons, which were essentially diffuse in structure, was the use of stories, or *exempla*, to illustrate a moral argument. 'The Nun's Priest's Tale' as a whole is an *exemplum*, and it contains within itself, as we have seen, a number of shorter *exempla*. Originality in the use of stories is not important. Neither is the truth of a tale, for medieval sermonists employed *exempla* not for their own sake, but as a means of reinforcing moral points in oral delivery. The literary importance of medieval *exempla* is emphasized by G. R. Owst:

> Preaching, and in especial the provision made for it in the way of collecting and preserving illustrative matter of all kinds, became the vehicle by which much of the lighter thought and imagination of antiquity—classical, oriental and early medieval—passed over into the thinking and writing of the modern world. Through the sermon, 'the short and farcical stories of common life' were elevated from the status of mere oral repetition to that of literature.[10]

His book demonstrates clearly the variety of these stories, and indicates many similarities with Chaucer's *exempla*. Of particular interest is part of a sermon attributed to Richard Alkerton:

> But that this be the more opyn, I put this ensaumple. I suppose that oure kyng hadde a certayn noumbre of knyʒtes to be feried over the se to a certayn ile, and thou comest and seist thou art a shipman, and undertakyst to brynge these men saf to the yle up-on peyne of outlawerie of his long and hongynge and drawynge, ʒif thou may be takyn; so that thei shul not perische be thi defaute or necgligence. And thou takist this ship with these knyʒtes, whos bodies the kyng chyargith more then al the temporal good of his reume. And when this ship is seylynge on the see in most pereiles, thou metyst with fischeris, and with hem thou dwellyst, and letist thi ship spille and hem that ben therinne. Whow darst thou evere se that kynges visage, whom thou hast so grevously despised and lost that he so tendirli lovyd?[11]

This short narrative is followed by a moral explanation in accordance with sermon convention, a pattern which Chaucer's usage closely follows. Another feature which we find in Chaucer's Tale

is the device of strengthening arguments by reference to authorities, most often drawn from the Bible or philosophical books:

> 'And forthermoore, I pray yow, looketh wel
> In the olde testament, of Daniel . . .'
>
> (3127–8)

and:

> 'But I ne kan nat bulte it to the bren
> As kan the hooly doctour Augustyn,
> Or Boece, or the Bisshop Bradwardyn . . .'
>
> (3240–2)

Nevill Coghill has noted no less than twenty-four references to different authors in the Tale.[12] It would appear, then, that the Nun's Priest is drawing on his preaching skill in the presentation of his Tale. Chaucer's voice, too, is present in some of the ecclesiastical material of the Tale, most notably in the satirical attitude implied in the Debate on Predestination.

The sound of Chauntecleer's crowing brings us back to the narrative. The drama and excitement are conveyed in the speed of the verse and in the hard, emphatic consonants of:

> And daun Russell the fox stirte up atones,
> And by the gargat hente Chauntecleer,
> And on his bak toward the wode hym beer,
> For yet ne was ther no man that hym sewed.
>
> (3334–7)

This is the climax of the Tale, and in order to emphasize the mock-heroic nature of the disaster Chaucer breaks off the narrative and presents a rhetorical sequence of address to Destiny and Venus, and finally to the author of a medieval textbook on the art of writing poetry, Gaufred or Geoffroi de Vinsauf:

> O Gaufred, deere maister soverayn,
> That whan thy worthy kyng Richard was slayn
> With shot, compleynedest his deeth so soore,
> Why ne hadde I now thy sentence and thy loore,
> The Friday for to chide, as diden ye?
> For on a Friday, soothly, slayn was he.
> Thanne wolde I shewe yow how that I koude pleyne
> For Chauntecleres drede and for his peyne.
>
> (3347–54)

Geoffroi's book *Nova Poetria* (New Poetry) was one of the most famous of medieval writings on the *ars poetica*, and as such it occupied an important place in schools in the Middle Ages.[13] Chaucer, of course, had been educated in this tradition, and it is clear that he knew about Geoffroi's ideas. Geoffroi's subject is the theory and practice of Rhetoric and his book not only lists rhetorical techniques, but also gives examples for the benefit of students. One of the most useful devices mentioned by Geoffroi is the *exclamatio* or *apostrophatio*, in which, at a moment of triumph or disaster, the poet addresses himself to Fortune or to a god. To illustrate this device, Geoffroi presents a number of examples in *Nova Poetria*, and one of these is a lament for the death of Richard I, who died on a Friday. The connection with Chaucer's passage is immediately clear, and the effect of his apostrophe to Gaufred is doubly humorous. It skilfully deflates the entire heroic build-up with which he has elaborately surrounded the catastrophe. And there is also a sense of light comedy in the disrespectful address to Geoffroi.

Chaucer's use of rhetorical techniques does not end here. It continues in the lamentation sequence, where Chaucer compares the grief and horror in the farmyard with the lament of the women of Troy:

> Certes, swich cry ne lamentacion,
> Was nevere of ladyes maad whan Ylion
> Was wonne, and Pirrus with his streite swerd,
> Whan he hadde hent kyng Priam by the berd,
> And slayn hym, as seith us *Eneydos*,
> As maden alle the hennes in the clos,
> Whan they had seyn of Chauntecleer the sighte.
>
> (3355–61)

Chaucer makes use of this same device in Dorigen's Complaint in 'The Franklin's Tale', and in 'The Merchant's Tale'. But here the effect is quite different, for in 'The Nun's Priest's Tale' Chaucer's dual focus makes this passage a parody. While he is building up the heroic dimension by his classical references, Chaucer is demolishing it by the exaggerated tone of the verse. We are, in fact, watching just a group of noisy hens:

> O woful hennes, right so criden ye,
> As, whan that Nero brende the citee

Of Rome, cryden senatoures wyves
For that hir husbondes losten alle hir lyves . . .

(3369–72)

This whole sequence is a parody, but Chaucer is not simply
laughing at rhetorical method in medieval poetry, for much of his
own poetry, especially his early work, makes full use of rhetorical
devices, and he learned a great deal from the instructions of a
work like *Nova Poetria*. One of the best examples of Chaucer's
unselfconsciously rhetorical early verse is the description of the
game of chess with Fortune in his *Book of the Duchess*:

'Allas! how myghte I fare werre?
My boldnesse ys turned to shame,
For fals Fortune hath pleyd a game
Atte ches with me, allas the while! . . .
With hir false draughtes dyvers
She staal on me, and tok my fers.
And whan I sawgh my fers awaye,
Allas! I kouthe no lenger playe,
But seyde, "Farewel, swete, ywys,
And farewel al that ever ther ys!"
Therwith Fortune seyde "Chek her!"
And "Mat!" in myd poynt of the chekker,
With a poun errant, allas!'

(616–19, 653–61)

The difference between this and 'The Nun's Priest's Tale' is one
of tone. The effect of Chaucer's later satirical approach is to
bring about an ironic reversal of attitude and judgement concerning literary form and, on a wider scale, general problems of
human life. The process is a fascinating one, the more so since
it is not simply negative and destructive, for the kind of parody
which we find here has a very real positive design. As such it
plays a major part in the wider view of satire outlined by
Northrop Frye:

The cultural effect of such satire is not to denigrate romance, but
to prevent any group of conventions from dominating the whole of
literary experience. Second-phase satire shows literature assuming
a special function of analysis, of breaking up the lumber of stereo-
types, fossilized beliefs, superstitious terrors, crank theories, pedantic
dogmatisms, oppressive fashions, and all other things that impede
the free movement (not necessarily, of course, the progress) of

society. Such satire is the completion of the logical process known as the *reductio ad absurdum*, which is not designed to hold one in perpetual captivity, but to bring one to the point at which one can escape from an incorrect procedure.[14]

'The Nun's Priest's Tale' itself employs many of the techniques recommended by Geoffroi. In addition to the lengthy *exempla* and *exclamationes* there are shorter examples occupying just a few lines, such as the apostrophe to traitors (lines 3226–9) and the proverbial concision of the *sententia*:

> Lo, how Fortune turneth sodeynly
> The hope and pryde eek of hir enemy!
> (3403–4)

The description of Chauntecleer at the beginning of the Tale follows closely Geoffroi's directions for *descriptio*:

> A summo capitis descendat splendor ad ipsam
> Radicem, totumque simul poliature ad unguem.[15]

and Chaucer does indeed begin at the top and work downwards:

> His coomb was redder than the fyn coral,
> And batailled as it were a castel wal;
> His byle was blak, and as the jeet it shoon;
> Lyk asure were his legges and his toon . . .
> (2859–62)

Another device recommended by Geoffroi is that of *collatio* which Chaucer employs when he compares the hens' cackling to the lamentations of the Roman women. Chaucer's attack, then, is not directed towards rhetorical method itself, but towards writers who were restricted by close adherence to rules at the expense of true feeling. His target once again is pedantry, while in a lighter vein he invites us simply to laugh at the incongruity of the high rhetorical style in a description of animals in a farmyard.

Just as the Tale began with a fine description of the widow and her situation, so now, as it draws to its conclusion, Chaucer produces a remarkable poetic effect as we watch the pursuit of the Fox down the forest glade. In both these passages, Chaucer's subject is not scholarly learning but the reality of country life, and his enthusiasm is apparent in the excited rhythm and the vivid sounds, colours and movements of the chase:

This sely wydwe and eek hir doghtres two
Herden thise hennes crie and maken wo,
And out at dores stirten they anon,
And syen the fox toward the grove gon,
And bar upon his bak the cok away,
And cryden, 'Out! harrow! and weylaway!
Ha! ha! the fox!' and after hym they ran,
And eek with staves many another man.
Ran Colle oure dogge, and Talbot and Gerland,
And Malkyn, with a dystaf in hir hand;
Ran cow and calf, and eek the verray hogges,
So fered for the berkyng of the dogges
And shoutyng of the men and wommen eeke,
They ronne so hem thoughte hir herte breeke.

(3375–88)

The repetition of 'and' and the simple vocabulary contribute to
the rhythmic pressure of the verse. The inclusion of blunt,
homely dialogue, and the variety of detail makes the whole
sequence come alive. Chaucer even makes a swarm of bees join
the chase! The effect is one of hilarious comedy and noisy
confusion. The language itself recreates the sounds of the farmyard:

Of bras they broghten bemes, and of box,
Of horn, of boon, in whiche they blewe and powped,
And therwithal they skriked and they howped.

(3398–400)

Detailed representation of this kind is common in medieval visual
art, especially in illuminated psalters and church carvings. In
fact, we may find scenes with a cock, fox and widow very similar
to Chaucer's carved beneath the misericords in Norwich Cathedral or the Parish Church at Boston in Lincolnshire.[16] But
although Chaucer may be drawing on a popular tradition and
technique, his creation is unique, for nothing can approach the
energy and realism of this passage.

The dramatic reversal of fortune with which the narrative ends
brings together a number of ideas found elsewhere in the Tale.
First, the epigrammatic couplet:

Lo, how Fortune turneth sodeynly
The hope and pryde eek of hir enemy!

(3403–4)

(another example of the rhetorical device of *sententia*) recalls the discussion on Predestination together with the insistent idea of chance in the first of Chauntecleer's tales. It also re-introduces the theme of pride and over-confidence. Chauntecleer can now recognize this as the cause of his own fall, and it is, ironically, the same vice in the Fox which he uses to secure his escape. In addition, the personality of the Nun's Priest plays a major role in linking the varied threads of the Tale. Towards the conclusion of the narrative he addresses himself directly to his congregation: 'Now, goode men, I prey yow herkneth alle' (3402), and references to God and the Bible become more frequent: 'God help me so!', 'God lat him nevere thee!' and 'seint Paul seith . . .'. Thus our attention focuses more and more closely on good sir John, and this is appropriate since the whole Tale is, as we have seen, based largely on the form of a conventional medieval sermon. When approached in this light, we see the importance of the insistent moralizing at the end of the Tale.

Our final question must concern the moral of the story. This is a problem which has occupied scholars at length, and many interesting readings have been put forward. Some concern traditional beast fables, and particularly the interpretation of the part played by the Fox. The most relevant to 'The Nun's Priest's Tale' is the idea of the Fox as a symbol of religious hypocrisy, a reading which adds considerable depth to the thread of satire against contemporary ecclesiastical practices which runs through the Tale. Chauntecleer would thus become the simple layman led astray by a corrupt church. Yet Chauntecleer is very far from being just a simple layman. He is a prince in his court, for Chaucer's poetry deliberately raises him to the heroic plain. And, at the same time, he is a chicken in a dusty farmyard.

Where, then, does Chaucer stand? To answer this we must return again to the design of the Tale as a whole. It is a work of brilliant variety and constantly changing focus, with many levels of reference. This is true, too, of its conclusion. There is a simple moral, explicitly presented by the Cock:

> 'For he that wynketh, whan he sholde see;
> Al wilfully, God lat him nevere thee!'
>
> (3431–2)

and the Priest:

> Lo, swich it is for to be recchelees
> And necligent, and truste on flaterye.
>
> (3436-7)

But this clearly cannot sum up the experience of the poem as a whole. Chaucer's voice is also present at the end of the Tale in the ambiguity of these lines:

> Taketh the moralite, goode men.
> For seint Paul seith that al that writen is,
> To oure doctrine it is ywrite, ywis;
> Taketh the fruyt, and lat the chaf be stille.
>
> (3440-3)

The suggestion here is that the moral of the story is not as straightforward as we might think at first. If we read the poem as a statement of one specific moral view, we limit Chaucer's design. For he is the total ironist, and as such he refuses to make it clear even that he is being ironic. We recognize the wit and humour of his verse; we observe and consider the many objects of his satire. But the poet's attitude seems to be in a state of constant flux, as the focus and perspective of the Tale changes. This is the technique of the true ironist who, as Northrop Frye says:

> deprecates himself and, like Socrates, pretends to know nothing, even that he is ironic. Complete objectivity and suppression of all explicit moral judgements are essential to his method. . . . When we try to isolate the ironic as such, we find that it seems to be simply the attitude of the poet as such, a dispassionate construction of a literary form, with all assertive elements, implied or expressed, eliminated . . . Irony is naturally a sophisticated mode, and the chief difference between sophisticated and naïve irony is that the naïve ironist calls attention to the fact that he is being ironic, whereas sophisticated irony merely states, and lets the reader add the ironic tone himself.[17]

It is, therefore, an individual response, not only at the conclusion, but throughout the Tale, which Chaucer invites, for this is a poem which raises searching questions about the nature of existence and man's response to the human predicament.

Conclusion

It would be quite wrong to consider the *Canterbury Tales* discussed in the foregoing chapters as isolated works. Each separate Tale must be examined in relation, not only to the complete body of Chaucer's own writing, but also to the whole literary tradition.

The essay on 'The General Prologue' endeavours to show how the Prologue, as well as providing a dramatic unifying theme for the publication of a collection of tales, also creates a unity among the apparently isolated portraits of the pilgrims themselves, which is in accord with medieval intellectual and philosophical thought. That this concept of Order in the Universe was applied to inanimate objects as well as to human beings is brought out in the discussion on the alchemy in 'The Canon's Yeoman's Tale'. Beauty, meaning conformity to an accepted pattern, was synonymous with Unity, and the same aesthetic unity in the portraits of the pilgrims in 'The General Prologue' is to be found in nearly all the Tales as the story-tellers reveal their characters as the narrative unfolds. The Miller and the Reeve are further obvious examples.

Linked to this aesthetic theory were the rules of rhetoric. Chaucer's use of the methods and devices of medieval rhetoric is fundamental to his verse, and so an appreciation of some of his best poetic effects demands some knowledge of the *artes poeticae* and *praedicandi*. It is true that the ironic tone of the Franklin's Prologue is easily recognizable, but the playful humour of the Nun's Priest at the climax of his Tale, or the tone and style of the whole of the Prioress's Tale will be lost, to a large extent, unless the reader is aware of the ideas of Geoffroi de Vinsauf and the forms and techniques of medieval preaching and popular religious literature. Such an understanding is essential for an appreciation of the lengthy digressions and lists of *exempla* to be found in the Tales of the Franklin, the Nun's Priest and the Pardoner.

The most important of all the literary theories and structures which influenced Chaucer was that of Courtly Love. He was, we know, well aware of the true position of women in England and western Europe during the Middle Ages. But like so many of his contemporaries, he was fascinated by the romantic ideas of *Amour Courtois*, which created a religion of love, and provided an elaborate system of rules and beliefs which offered some alternative to the darker reality of the human predicament. This is not escapism, however, for the Courtly Love tradition

provided Chaucer with a framework within which he could explore in great depth the mysteries of human relationships. Chaucer's essentially realistic attitude to the Courtly Love tradition is most clearly represented during the course of the Marriage Debate which is sparked off by the Wife of Bath's outspokenly feminist view that the wife should be the dominant partner in any marriage. The chapter on 'The Clerk's Tale' discusses the way in which the Clerk replies to the Wife with a story of an exceptionally domineering husband. 'The Merchant's Tale' also plays an integral part in the argument, which Chaucer finally resolves in 'The Franklin's Tale' by advocating a compromise between the extremes of the rigid application of the rules of *Amour Courtois* and the practicalities of daily life.

This tradition is at the heart of Chaucer's earlier work *Troilus and Criseyde* and it influences the behaviour of the courtly lovers in 'The Knight's Tale'. Chaucer was not alone in finding in this tradition a philosophy and a literary structure of absorbing interest, but among his contemporaries, only the unknown poet of *Sir Gawain and the Green Knight* came near to equalling his achievement.

We know that Chaucer read widely in philosophical and theological books. In particular he learned much from other European writers, and his travels, especially in Italy, provided vital opportunities for the pursuit of such comparative studies. Some of the essays in this book have tried to show how Chaucer evaluates this knowledge as he draws freely on the material and ideas of contemporary and earlier writers, and tests out traditional and revolutionary theories about life and art. We have already noted this kind of evaluation in 'The Franklin's Tale', where Chaucer advocated a middle course between the extreme arguments over marriage. Concerning theological problems he adopts a similar position in the arguments over Pre-destination and Free Will, which he examines with characteristic clarity and economy in 'The Nun's Priest's Tale'. Here Chaucer acknowledges the profound influence of Boethius, who tried to reconcile these two arguments in the *Consolatione Philosophiae* which Chaucer translated into his *Boece*. It is Boethian philosophy also which provides the philosophical thought of *Troilus and Criseyde* and 'The Knight's Tale', and it provides the literary authority for such dignified invocations as are found in 'The Franklin's Tale'.

Chaucer shares with his contemporaries a deep interest in the beliefs, traditions and organization of the medieval Church. Some of the servants of the Church in Chaucer's day were men of moral stature who committed themselves conscientiously to the duties of their calling; the Parson who rides on the pilgrimage is such a man. Others were much less concerned with pastoral or spiritual affairs, and the rich worldliness

of clerics like the Monk stirred Chaucer's indignation. As for the lay hangers-on like the Pardoner and the Summoner, their activities must have represented with compelling force the corruption which lay close to the heart of the medieval Church. Yet Chaucer's satire is tempered with the fine humour which characterizes the whole of the *Canterbury Tales*. It is this tone which basically distinguishes his satire from that of his contemporary William Langland, who was guided in *Piers Plowman* by a much sterner vision which utterly condemned the shortcomings of churchmen and laiety alike.

Chaucer constantly searches behind the surface of life as he attempts to reach his own assessment of human problems and the meaning of existence, but this never blinds him to the realities of human experience. His preoccupation with religious thinking and his concern for the state of the Church reflects the precariousness of life in his day and is to be found most noticeably in the portraits of the characters of religion among the pilgrims in 'The General Prologue' and in the Tales of the Nun's Priest and the Pardoner, both of whom tell stories of violence with the threat of impending doom ever hanging over the central characters.

For much of his life Chaucer was actively engaged in public service. His experience as a civil servant and Member of Parliament gave him considerable insight into the economic and commercial developments of his day, and his knowledge of these affairs gives added perspective to much of his writing. Two socio-economic problems in particular engaged Chaucer's interest and sympathy, and his concern for them is often reflected in the *Canterbury Tales*. One is the extreme material poverty which many of the lower classes suffered (a situation which was aggravated by the fraudulent exploitation of the ignorant poor by officers of the Church and lay landowners alike). Enlightened thinkers condemned such oppression, and here Chaucer has much in common again with Langland in the depth of his compassion for the squalid and painful situation of so many fellow human beings. 'The Nun's Priest's Tale' provides an ironic social study of contemporary life emphasizing as it does this contrast between the squalor and colourless existence of the widow, and the colourful regal splendour of Chauntecleer; but it is, of course, not the 'sely wydwe' but Chauntecleer who, in spite of all his nobility and learning, comes to grief and is beguiled by the Fox. This is doubly ironic when one realizes that here is Chaucer, the courtier, telling the story to a sophisticated court audience. Chaucer was also concerned with the effects of disease on England and its people in the Middle Ages. The economic structure of medieval life was cracked and distorted by the depopulation and devastation caused by plague and famine, and, although medical research sought to offer the

possibility of cure and progress, there was little, in fact, that could be done. Chaucer followed closely the activities of physicians and re-searchers in other branches of science, and he must have hoped for advances in this field comparable to the progress which he witnessed in the fields of trade and commercial law and organization. There is abundant evidence in all his works of his wide reading and absorbing interest in the scientific developments of his time. His description in 'The General Prologue' of his Doctor of Physik shows his knowledge of medical history and in 'The Nun's Priest's Tale' and 'The Knight's Tale' he reveals his understanding of the medical lore of the Middle Ages and his acquaintance with contemporary surgical methods. The Canon's Yeoman takes us right inside the chemistry laboratory and we are aware of the close affinity between this branch of science and the whole range of philosophical thought.

This kind of evidence testifies to Chaucer's lively interest in every aspect of human affairs and ideas. He communicates his interest and insight through his style, and it is to this aspect of his work that we must return in conclusion. The essential quality of his poetic genius is its great versatility; it ranges from formal simplicity to coarse ri-baldry, and from rapid dialogue to elaborate patterned descriptions. This variety of tone and language and rhythm and image recreates all the involved excitement of Chaucer's attitude to medieval life. Above all, it conveys his essential identification with his fellow human beings, and it is the warmth of this compassion, with his skill as a poet and story-teller, which makes Chaucer conspicuous among the writers of the Middle Ages, and which has made his work so rewarding over the years.

Notes

All quotations are taken from *The Works of Geoffrey Chaucer* ed. F. N. Robinson, 2nd ed. (London 1957) (Boston: Houghton Mifflin, 1957).

THE GENERAL PROLOGUE

1. Friedrich Heer, *The Intellectual History of Europe*, trans. Jonathan Steinberg (London 1966), p. 153.
2. Erwin Panofsky, *Gothic Architecture and Scholasticism* (London 1957) (New York: New American Library).
3. Friedrich Heer, op. cit., p. 153.
4. Przemyslaw Mroczkowski, "Mediaeval Art and Aesthetics in The Canterbury Tales," *Speculum* xxxiii (1958), pp. 204–21.
5. Northrop Frye, *Anatomy of Criticism: Four Essays* (Princeton: Princeton University Press, 1957), p. 311.
6. Henry Adams, *Mont-St-Michel and Chartres* (Washington 1904) (New York: Mentor Books, 1961), p. 369.
7. James Sutherland, *A Preface to Eighteenth Century Poetry* (Oxford and New York: Oxford University Press, 1948), p. 117.
8. James Sutherland, op. cit., p. 109.
9. Arthur W. Hoffman, "Chaucer's Prologue to Pilgrimage: the Two Voices" reprinted from *ELH* xxi (1954), pp. 1-16 in *Chaucer: Modern Essays in Criticism*, ed. Edward Wagenknecht (New York: Oxford University Press, 1959).
10. John Speirs, *Chaucer the Maker*, 2nd ed. (London 1960) (Bridgeport, CT: Merrimack Publishing, 1964).
11. *Chaucer's Poetry: An Anthology for the Modern Reader*, ed. E. T. Donaldson (New York: Ronald Press, 1958), p. 876.
12. Charles Muscatine, "The Canterbury Tales: Style of the Man and Style of the Work" in *Chaucer and Chaucerians: Critical Studies in Middle English Literature*, ed. D. S. Brewer (London 1966), p. 99.
13. *English Critical Essays: Sixteenth, Seventeenth, and Eighteenth Centuries*, ed. E. D. Jones (London 1922) (New York: Oxford University Press).
14. See also Nevill Coghill, *The Poet Chaucer* (London 1949), p. 116 ff (Philadelphia, PA: R. West, 1950).
15. For a historical description see W. A. Pantin, *The English Church in the Fourteenth Century* (Cambridge 1955) (Toronto: University of Toronto Press, 1980).

16. *The Vision of William concerning Piers the Plowman*, ed. Walter W. Skeat (Oxford 1886) B Text, Passus v, 409-10 (New York: Oxford University Press, 1924).

17. See also Arthur W. Hoffman, art. cit., p. 30.

18. J. Huizinga, *The Waning of the Middle Ages: a Study of the Forms of Life, Thought and Art in France and the Netherlands in the XIVth and XVth Centuries*, trans. F. Hopman (London 1924) (Harmondsworth: Penguin Books, 1955), p. 124, (New York: St. Martin's Press, 1924).

19. See Ralph Baldwin, *The Unity of the Canterbury Tales*, *Anglistica V* (Copenhagen 1955) (Folcroft, PA: Folcroft Library Editions, 1955).

THE KNIGHTS TALE

In addition to the works listed below I am particularly indebted to the scholarly essay by Elizabeth Salter in her *Chaucer: The Knight's Tale and The Clerk's Tale* (London 1962).

1. Boethius, *Quomodo substantiae*, in *Boethius: The Theological Tractates and The Consolation of Philosophy*, trans. H. F. Stewart (London 1918) quoted in Anne Fremantle, *The Age of Belief: the Medieval Philosophers* (New York: New American Library, 1955), pp. 56 and 65.

2. See also Charles Muscatine, "Form, Texture and Meaning in Chaucer's Knight's Tale," reprinted from *PMLA* lxv (1950) pp. 911-29 in *Chaucer: Modern Essays in Criticism*, ed. Edward Wagenknecht (New York: Oxford University Press, 1959).

3. See also Gervase Mathew, *The Court of Richard II* (London 1968), chapters xiv and xv.

4. Friedrich Heer, *The Intellectual History of Europe*, trans. cit. p. 155.

5. Charles Muscatine, art. cit. p. 81.

THE TALES OF THE PRIORESS AND THE CLERK

1. Be bold and be patient, in pain and in joy,
   for he that rends his clothes too rashly
   must sit anon in worse to sew them together.
   Wherefore when poverty presses me and pains enow,
   calmly in sufferance it behoves me be patient;
   despite penance and pain, to prove to men's sight
   that patience is a noble point, though it oft displease.
   Patience, ed. I. Gollancz (London 1924)

2. The Synagogue, Rochester Cathedral, reproduced in G. G. Coulton, *Medieval Panorama: the English Scene from Conquest to Reformation* (Cambridge 1938) (New York: Norton, 1974).

3. The Rochester sculpture is paralleled by a remarkably similar one in Strasbourg Cathedral, reproduced in Friedrich Heer, *The Medieval World: Europe 1100-1350*, trans. Janet Sondheimer (London 1962) (New York: Norton: 1974).

4. F. Pollock and F. W. Maitland, *The History of English Law before the Time of Edward I*, quoted in G. G. Coulton, op. cit., p. 349.

5. See Marie Padgett Hamilton, "Echoes of Childermass in the Tale of the Prioress," reprinted from *The Modern Language Review* xxxiv (1939), pp. 1–8 in *Chaucer: Modern Essays in Criticism*, ed. Edward Wagenknecht (New York: Oxford University Press, 1959).

6. K. Young, *The Drama of the Medieval Church* (Oxford and New York: Oxford University Press, 1933), vol. i, p. 110.

7. *Pearl*, ed. E. V. Gordon (Oxford 1953) (New York: Oxford University Press, 1963).

8. Quoted in Friedrich Heer, *The Medieval World: Europe 1100-1350*, trans. cit., p. 322

9. There is an interesting chapter on the life of medieval women in G. G. Coulton, op. cit., pp. 614-28.

10. See *The Paston Letters*, ed. J. Fenn and L. Archer-Hind (London 1924).

11. When I see flowers begin to grow and hear the song of birds, my heart is pierced completely by a sweet lover's yearning for a new love that is so sweet and true that it gladdens all my singing. I know surely that all my joy and my happiness is caused wholly by him (i.e. Christ).
This passage is the opening stanza of "A Spring Song on the Passion," no 18 of *The Harley Lyrics: the Middle English Lyrics of MS. Harley 2253, 3rd ed.* (Manchester 1964) (New York: Barnes & Noble, 1964).

12. The few short sections of "The Clerk's Tale" written in Chaucer's later style are subsequent additions to the poem (viz: The Prologue ll. 995-1000 and the Clerk's Envoy ll. 1163-1212).

13. This problem is discussed at length in an excellent essay on "The Clerk's Tale" by Elizabeth Salter in her *Chaucer: The Knight's Tale and The Clerk's Tale* (London 1962).

THE CANON'S YEOMAN'S TALE

1. See the argument by Marie P. Hamilton, "The Clerical Status of Chaucer's Alchemist," *Speculum* xvi (1941), pp. 103-8, referred to in Robinson's ed., p. 760.

2. See the note on "The Canon's Yeoman's Tale" in Robinson's ed., p. 759.

3. Much of Chaucer's wide knowledge of alchemy was collected from the authoritative work by Vincent de Beauvais in *Speculum*

Naturale, the first great medieval encyclopedia.
4. Friedrich Heer, *The Intellectual History of Europe*, trans. cit.,
   p. 153.
5. Cf. "The Nun's Priest's Tale," ll. 3063-3104.
6. Fourteen of the pilgrims end their tales with a benediction of some
   kind, viz: the Knight, the Miller, the Reeve, the Man of Law, the
   Wife of Bath, the Friar, the Merchant, the Pardoner, the Shipman,
   the Prioress, Chaucer himself (in the Tale of Melibee), the Nun's
   Priest, the Canon's Yeoman and the Parson.

THE FRANKLIN'S TALE

A special note of acknowledgment must be made to the two editions
of the Franklin's Tale, by Phyllis Hodgson (London 1960) (Atlantic
Highlands, NJ: Humanities Press, 1960) and by A. C. Spearing (Cambridge and New York: Cambridge University Press, 1966), to both of
which this chapter owes a good deal.

1. G. L. Kittredge, "Chaucer's Discussion of Marriage," reprinted
   from *Modern Philology* ix (1911-1912), pp. 435-467 in *Chaucer:
   Modern Essays in Criticism*, ed. Edward Wagenknecht (New York:
   Oxford University Press, 1959).
2. Northrop Frye, op. cit., p. 96.
3. C. S. Lewis, *The Allegory of Love: a Study in Medieval Tradition*
   (Oxford and New York: Oxford University Press, 1936), pp. 2-3.
4. Charles Muscatine, "The Canterbury Tales: Style of the Man and
   Style of the Work," in *Chaucer and Chaucerians: Critical Studies
   in Middle English Literature*, ed. D. S. Brewer (London 1966),
   pp. 102-3 (University, AL: University of Alabama Press, 1966).
5. Introduction to *The Franklin's Prologue and Tale*, ed. A. C.
   Spearing (Cambridge and New York: Cambridge University Press,
   1966), p. 21.
6. James Sledd, "Dorigen's Complaint," *Modern Philology* xlv (1947-
   1948), pp. 36-45.
7. See also A. C. Spearing, ed. cit., pp. 22-38 for a detailed and interesting consideration of the themes of 'Trouthe', Marriage and
   'Gentillesse' in the tale.
8. Ibid., p. 32.
9. *Chaucer: The Franklin's Tale*, ed. Phyllis Hodgson (London 1960),
   p. 136. (Atlantic Highlands, NJ: Humanities Press, 1960).
10. A. C. Spearing, ed. cit., p. 54.
11. Nevill Coghill, "Chaucer's Narrative Art in The Canterbury
    Tales," in *Chaucer and Chaucerians: Critical Studies in Middle
    English Literature*, ed. D. S. Brewer (London 1966), p. 136
    (University, AL: University of Alabama Press, 1966).
12. G. L. Kittredge, art. cit., p. 211.

13. G. T. Shepherd, "Troilus and Criseyde," in *Chaucer and Chaucerians: Critical Studies in Middle English Literature*, ed. D. S. Brewer (London 1966), p. 74 (University, AL: University of Alabama Press, 1966).

14. Nevill Coghill, *The Poet Chaucer*, op. cit., p. 171.

15. Ibid., p. 170.

THE PARDONER'S TALE

1. J. Huizinga, op. cit., p. 134.

2. See *Sermo Lupi ad Anglos*, ed. Dorothy Whitelock, 3rd ed. (London 1963) (Atlantic Highlands, NJ: Humanities Press, 1980).

3. G. G. Coulton, op. cit., p. 505.

4. See Walter Clyde Curry, *Chaucer and the Medieval Sciences*, 2nd ed. (London 1960).

5. There prechede a pardoner as he a prest were
   And brouht forth a bulle with a bischopis selys,
   Sayde that hymself myhte assoylen hem alle
   Of falsnesses and fastynges, of vowes ybrokene.
   Lewed men leved hym wel and lykede his wordes
   And comen and knelede to kyss en his bulles;
   He bounchede hem with his brevet and blered here yes
   And raughte with his rageman rynges and broches.
   Thus ye gyve youre gold, glotons to helpe,
   And leneth it lorelles that lecherye haunten.
   Were the bischop yblessed and worth bothe his eres,
   His seel sholde nought be ysent in deseyte of the people.
   Ac it is nought by the bischop, I leve, that the boy precheth,
   For the parsche-prest and the pardoner parten the selver
   That the peple in parsches sholde have, yf thei ne were.
   Piers the Plowman, C. Text, Passus I, ll. 66–80

6. The Pardoner claims that he was "aboute to wedde a wyf." See the Wife of Bath's Prologue, ll. 163-8.

7. G. R. Owst, *Literature and Pulpit in Medieval England: a Neglected Chapter in the History of English Letters & of the English People*, 2nd ed. (Oxford 1961) (New York: Barnes & Noble, 1966).

8. This is discussed at greater length in chapters 5 and 7 on "The Franklin's Tale" and "The Nun's Priest's Tale."

9. This figure occurs in *Piers the Plowman*, C Text, Passus xxiii, ll. 220-28 (see epigraph to this chapter).

10. See chapter 4 note 6

11. This painting by Grünewald forms one of the wings of the Isenheim altar-piece.

THE NUN'S PRIEST'S TALE

1. On sources see *Sources and Analogues of Chaucer's Canterbury Tales,* ed. W. F. Bryan and Germaine Dempster (Chicago 1941) (Atlantic Highlands, NJ: Humanities Press, 1958).
2. "Monster," she said, "fly away! Indeed, the sight of you offends me so much that I very often abandon my song because of your foul appearance. My heart sinks and my tongue falters when you are close to me."
3. G. R. Owst, *Literature and Pulpit in Medieval England,* ed. cit., p. 205.
4. Ibid., p. 198.
5. See the essay by David Holbrook in *A Guide to English Literature,* ed. Boris Ford, vol. I, *The Age of Chaucer,* rev. ed. (Harmondsworth 1961) (New York: Penguin, 1965).
6. See G. L. Kittredge, art. cit.
7. G. R. Owst, op. cit., p. 387.
8. See J. Huizinga, op. cit, especially chapter 8, "Love Formalised"
9. The colours attributed to Chauntecleer and the Fox are similar to those in the coats of arms of Henry Bolingbroke and Thomas Mowbray, Earl Marshal of England, respectively. On this evidence it has been suggested that the Tale might have had the added excitement of a *roman à clef* for Chaucer's readers: see J. Leslie Hotson, "Colfax *vs.* Chauntecleer," reprinted from *PMLA* xxxix (1924) pp. 762–81 in *Chaucer: Modern Essays in Criticism,* ed. Edward Wagenknecht (New York: Oxford University Press 1959); and John Matthews Manly, *Some New Light on Chaucer: Lectures Delivered at the Lowell Institute.* (New York 1926) (*reprint.* Teaneck, NJ: Somerset Publishing).
10. G. R. Owst, op. cit., p. 207.
11. Ibid., pp. 177–8.
12. Nevill Coghill, op. cit.
13. A good analysis of the art of poetry in the middle ages is to be found in A. C. Spearing, *Criticism and Medieval Poetry,* (London 1964), pp. 46–67 (New York: Barnes & Noble, 1972); see also D. W. Robertson, *A Preface to Chaucer: Studies in Medieval Perspectives* (London 1963).
14. See Northrop Frye, op. cit., p. 233.
15. Let the glory (of her description) descend from the top of the head to the root itself, and, at the same time, let all be polished to the nail (i.e. completely).
16. See M. D. Anderson, *Misericords: Medieval Life in English Woodcarving* (Harmondsworth 1954).
17. Northrop Frye, op. cit., pp. 40–41.

Select Bibliography

EDITIONS

The Works of Geoffrey Chaucer, ed. F. N. Robinson, 2nd ed. (London 1957) (Boston: Houghton Mifflin, 1957).

The General Prologue to the Canterbury Tales, ed. James Winny (Cambridge and New York: Cambridge University Press, 1965)

The Clerk's Prologue and Tale, ed. James Winny (Cambridge and New York: Cambridge University Press, 1966).

The Canon's Yeoman's Prologue and Tale, ed. Maurice Hussey (Cambridge and New York: Cambridge University Press, 1966)

The Franklin's Prologue and Tale, ed. A. C. Spearing (Cambridge and New York: Cambridge University Press, 1965)

The Franklin's Tale, ed. Phyllis Hodgson (London 1960) (Atlantic Highlands, NJ: Humanities Press, 1960).

The Pardoner's Prologue and Tale, ed. A. C. Spearing (Cambridge 1965) (New York: Cambridge University Press, 1966).

The Nun's Priest's Prologue and Tale, ed. Maurice Hussey (Cambridge 1965) (New York: Cambridge University Press, 1966).

CRITICISM

A. C. Spearing's *Criticism and Medieval Poetry* (London 1964) (New York: Barnes & Noble, 1972) is invaluable to every student of medieval literature. Chaucer's connections with the literature of medieval France are discussed at length in Charles Muscatine's *Chaucer and the French Tradition: a study in Style and Meaning* (Berkeley: University of California Press, 1957). Further critical comment may be found in Nevill Coghill's *The Poet Chaucer* (London 1949) (Philadelphia, PA: R. West, 1950) and John Speirs's *Chaucer the Maker* (2nd ed., London 1960) (Bridgeport, CT: Merrimack Publishing, 1964). The introduction to E. T. Donaldson's anthology *Chaucer's Poetry: an Anthology for the Modern Reader* (New York: Ronald Press, 1958) is useful, and there are two excellent collections of essays, *Chaucer: Modern Essays in Criticism* ed. Edward Wagenknecht (New York: Oxford University Press, 1959), and *Chaucer and Chaucerians: Critical Studies in Middle English Literature*, ed. D. S. Brewer (London 1966). Elizabeth Salter's short study, *Chaucer: the Knight's Tale and the Clerk's Tale* (London 1962) develops some interesting critical ideas. There is a good recent critical account of

Chaucer's work, including the Dream Poems, *Troilus and Criseyde* and the *Canterbury Tales*, by John Lawlor in his *Chaucer* (London 1968).

BACKGROUND READING

The best readable account of life and thought in the late Middle Ages is still J. Huizinga's *The Waning of the Middle Ages* (London 1924) (New York: St. Martin's Press, 1924).

H. S. Bennett's *Life on the English Manor: a Study of Peasant Conditions 1150–1400* (Cambridge 1937) (New York: Cambridge University Press, 1960) is valuable for its insight into the social organization and customs of everyday life in the Middle Ages. G. G. Coulton's *Medieval Panorama* (Cambridge 1938) (New York: Norton, 1974) also contains useful information about many aspects of medieval life. The ideas and beliefs of European intellectuals in Chaucer's day may best be studied in Friedrich Heer's *The Medieval World* (London 1962) and Anne Fremantle's *The Age of Belief* (New York: New American Library, 1955).

FURTHER READING

J. L. Lowes, *Geoffrey Chaucer* (London 1934) (New York: Oxford University Press, 1934).

H. S. Bennett, *Chaucer and the Fifteenth Century* (Oxford and New York: Oxford University Press, 1947).

D. S. Brewer, *Chaucer in his Time* (London 1964) (New York: Longman, 1973).

Friedrich Heer, *The Intellectual History of Europe* (London 1966).

C. S. Lewis, *The Allegory of Love* (Oxford and New York: Oxford University Press, 1936).

G. R. Owst, *Literature and the Pulpit in the Middle Ages*, 2nd ed. (Oxford 1961) (New York: Barnes & Noble, 1966).

Gervase Mathew, *The Court of Richard II* (London 1968).

Henry Adams, *Mont-St-Michel and Chartres* (New York: Mentor Books, 1961).

Index